p.23

p.26

They go to the **library**.

They go to the **vet clinic**.

They go to the **fire station**.

They go to the **police station**.

p.39

p.42

We have a big living room.

We have a small bathroom.

We have a sunny kitchen.

We have three bedrooms.

p.55

p.58

But I can still have fun inside.

I fly my **kite** in the sky.

It's **sunny** today.

It's fun to play in the snow.

책 속 음원
바로 듣기!

음원 듣기 & 단어챈트 영상

남다른 학습법으로
기적 같은 실력을 보장하는

기적의 영어리딩

체계적인 6단계 커리큘럼

	1 with 파닉스	2 with 주제 어휘	3 with 문장 패턴
목표	큰소리 리딩으로 문자 해독력을 높여요	리딩의 재미를 알며 기초 어휘력을 쌓아요	필수 문형을 접하며 문장 이해력을 높여요
리딩 소스	일상 이야기, 만화, 동화, 서사 논픽션 읽기	일상 이야기, 만화, 동화, 서사 논픽션 읽기	초대장, 포스터, 규칙 등의 정보·지식이 결합된 스토리 읽기
난이도	AR 0.5~1.0 Lexile BR~50 Words 50~70 (6p)	AR 0.7~1.5 Lexile 25~200 Words 70~90 (6p)	AR 1.3~2.3 Lexile 125~400 Words 90~110 (4p)
성취 수준	기초 어휘 180개	초등 3~4학년 교과서 수준 필수 어휘 180개	초등 5~6학년 교과서 수준 필수 어휘 200개

✓ 독해력 성장의 핵심 과정을 탄탄하게 밟아가는 6단계 리딩 프로그램

✓ 기적만의 3-Step 완전학습 시스템으로 확실한 학습 성과를 보장!

✓ 새 교육과정을 연계한 콘텐츠로 리딩 기초부터 중학 수준까지 저절로 완성!

✓ 적정 학습분량과 친절한 학습안내로 혼자서도 끝까지 완주 가능

4 with 문장 구조

다양한 글감을 읽으며 문장 구성력을 키워요
일상 소재의 실용문, 짧은 논픽션 읽기
AR 2.3~3.3 Lexile 420~620 Words 100~130
고학년 독해력 완성

5 with 문법

글을 논리적으로 이해하여 핵심을 파악해요
교과 연계된 최신 소재의 정보글 읽기
AR 3.0~3.9 Lexile 550~680 Words 130~150
예비중 리딩 · 문법 통합

6 with 서술형 영작

읽은 내용을 바탕으로 정리하는 표현력을 길러요
교과 연계된 최신 소재의 정보글, 의견글 읽기
AR 3.7~4.7 Lexile 650~780 Words 150~180
중학 독해 · 서술형 시험 대비

리딩 첫 시작부터 독해력 완성까지!

기본 다지기 — 영어와 친해지는 스토리 리딩으로 기본 바탕을 튼튼히!

Level 1
Level 2
Level 3

기적의 영어리딩 Level 1~3

- 초등 저학년의 영어 성장을 위한 리딩 기초 학습서
- 일상 이야기, 카툰, 동화 등 흥미로운 스토리로 리딩을 즐겁게 시작
- 따라가면 저절로 학습이 완성되는 3-STEP(읽기-이해-확장) 매일 학습
- 리딩의 기본기를 탄탄히 하는 파닉스 → 어휘 → 문장을 순차적으로 강화

실력 완성하기 — 논픽션 리딩으로 읽고 이해하고 표현하는 힘 기르기!

기적의 영어리딩 Level 4~6

- 초등 고학년의 문해력 완성과 중학 영어로의 연결을 돕는 리딩 심화 학습서
- 다양한 실용문과 정보글을 읽으며 글의 구조를 시각화하고 핵심을 파악하는 힘 강화
- 읽은 내용을 바탕으로 정리하고 표현하는 서술형 영작 훈련
- 문장 구조 → 논리적 이해 → 표현력 확장으로 이어지는 단계별 아웃풋 설계

p.75

p.78

Put it on the bread.

Add some **tomatoes**.

First, toast two slices of bread.

Press gently and cut it in half.

p.91

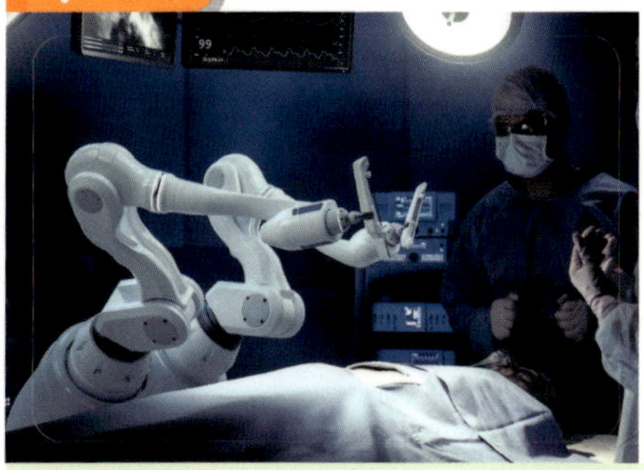

p.94

Robots can take orders.

They can help **doctors**.

Robots can **clean** the house.

Robots can build **cars**.

p.107

p.110

Now Beaky has some **flour**.

"No, you will not.

The **wheat** grows tall.

2C

짧은 문장 읽기
AR 0.7~1.5

기적의 영어리딩

with 주제 어휘

길벗스쿨

기적만의

3-Step 완전학습 시스템

읽고, 이해하고, 확장하는 3-Step 시스템으로 겉핥기가 아닌 진짜 실력을 키웁니다. 하나의 지문을 3단계에 걸쳐 깊이 있게 학습하면서 콘텐츠를 제대로 소화합니다. 동시에, 리딩의 기본 바탕이 되는 파닉스-어휘력-문장력을 차례로 강화합니다. 단순한 읽기를 넘어 문해력 성장을 위한 핵심 학습이 통합적으로 이루어지는 학습법입니다.

Step 1. 읽기

단어 익히기

스토리 지문을 이해하는 데 필수적인 키워드를 먼저 학습합니다.

스토리 리딩

몰입하여 즐길 수 있는 흥미로운 스토리를 담아, 반복하여 듣고 읽는 동안 단어와 표현을 쉽게 체화합니다.

Step 2. 이해

내용 확인 문제

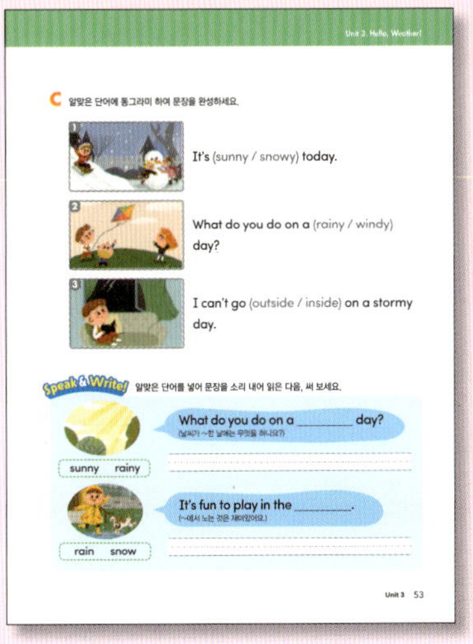

다양한 유형의 문제를 통해 읽은 내용을 충분히 이해하고, 단어 및 문장을 반복 학습하게 됩니다.

Step 3. 확장

주제 어휘 학습

실력을 한층 더 성장시키는 확장 학습 단계입니다.
Level 2에서는 스토리 주제와 연관된 단어들을 추가로 익히며 어휘량을 풍부하게 늘려 갑니다.

Contents

Level 2-C

✦ How to Study ✦

재미있는 스토리를 읽으며
주제별 어휘와 기초 문형으로 독해의 기초를 다집니다!

Level 2는 학습자가 흥미를 이어갈 수 있도록 스토리 기반 지문으로 구성하였습니다. 다양한 일러스트가 내용을 쉽게 이해하도록 도와주며, 반복해서 등장하는 문장 패턴을 통해 기초 문형을 자연스럽게 익힐 수 있습니다.

독해 실력을 키우는 첫걸음은 풍부한 어휘력에 있습니다. Level 2에서는 초기 학습자가 꼭 알아야 할 기초 단어에 더해 주제별 어휘까지 확장하여 어휘량을 풍부하게 늘리도록 합니다. 즐겁게 스토리를 따라 읽으며 기초 문형과 어휘력, 두 가지를 동시에 잡아 보세요.

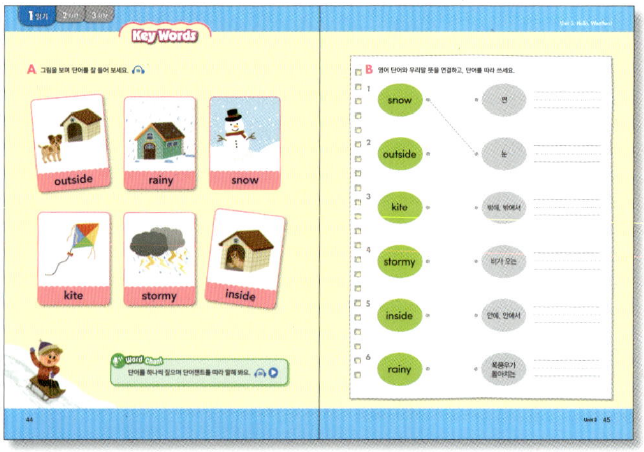

Step 1. 읽기
핵심 단어를 익힌 다음 지문 따라 읽기

❶ **[Key Words]**에서 핵심 단어의 발음을 듣고 뜻과 철자를 익혀요.

❷ 신나는 **[단어 챈트]**를 반복해서 들으며 단어를 확실히 익혀요.

❸ 간단한 액티비티를 풀며 단어를 즐겁게 복습해요.

❹ 세 가지 버전의 Read Aloud 가이드 음원을 들으며, 스토리 지문을 듣고 따라 읽어요.

[스토리 듣기] 오디오를 잘 들으며 어떤 내용인지 살펴봐요.

[집중 듣기] 손가락으로 하나씩 짚으며 글자에 집중하여 들어요.

[따라 읽기] 직접 소리내어 읽어봐요. 들려주는 문장을 한 줄씩 따라 읽어보세요.

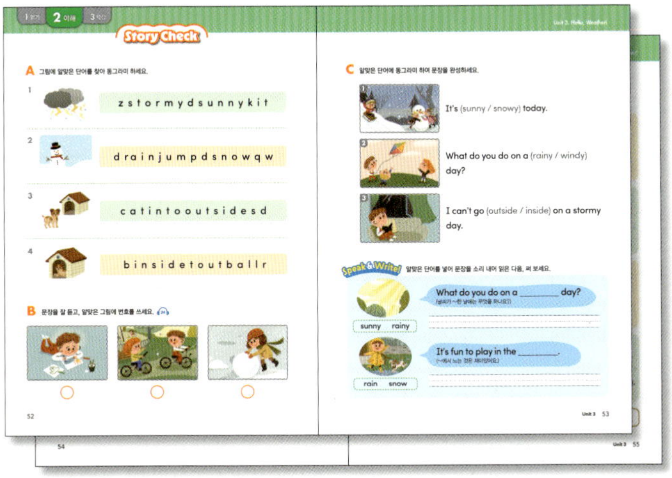

Step 2. 이해
문제를 풀며 지문을 제대로 이해하기

❶ [Story Check]에서는 여러 유형의 문제를 풀며 스토리의 흐름과 내용을 제대로 이해해요. 문제 속에서 단어와 문장을 반복해 만나며 영어표현을 자연스럽게 익혀요.

❷ 문제 풀이 후 **[별책]** 정답지를 참고하여 채점하고 틀린 문제를 확인해요.

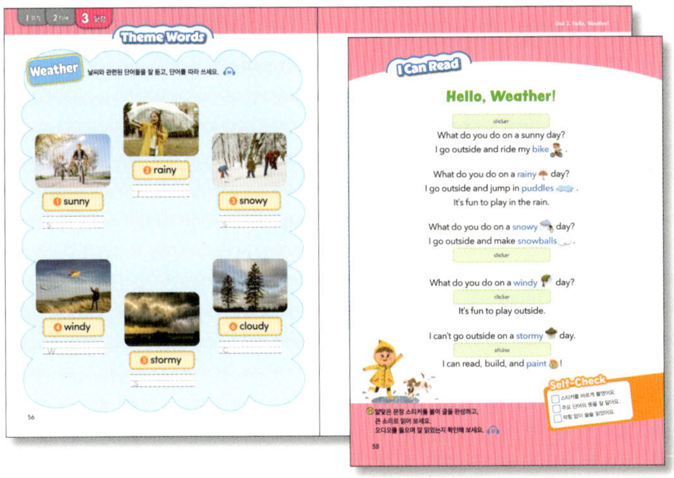

Step 3. 확장
주제별 어휘 학습 후, 스스로 소리내어 읽기

❶ [Theme Words]에서, 주제 연관 단어를 추가 학습합니다.

❷ 단어의 뜻과 철자 쓰기를 연습한 다음, 배운 단어를 활용해 내 생각을 표현해 봅니다.

❸ [I Can Read] 스스로 소리 내어 읽기 연습을 해요. 직접 소리내서 읽을수록 리딩 실력이 좋아집니다.

[Review Test] 리뷰 테스트 2회분이 포함됩니다. Unit 1~3에 대한 테스트와 Unit 4~6에 대한 테스트로 영어 실력을 확인해 볼 수 있어요.

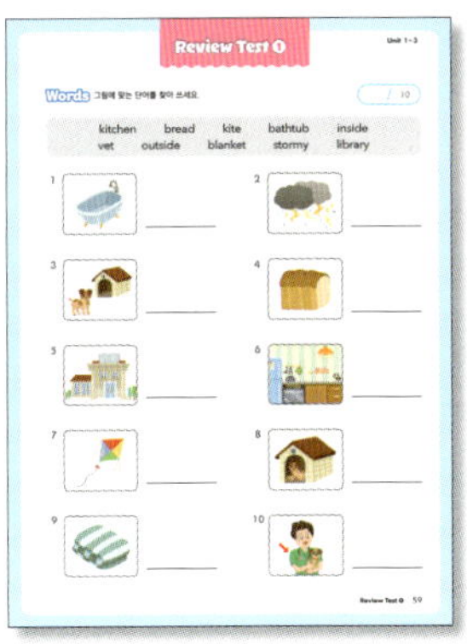

[별책: Practice Book] 단어·문장 쓰기, 딕테이션, 주제 어휘에 관련해 선택적으로 보충학습을 할 수 있습니다.

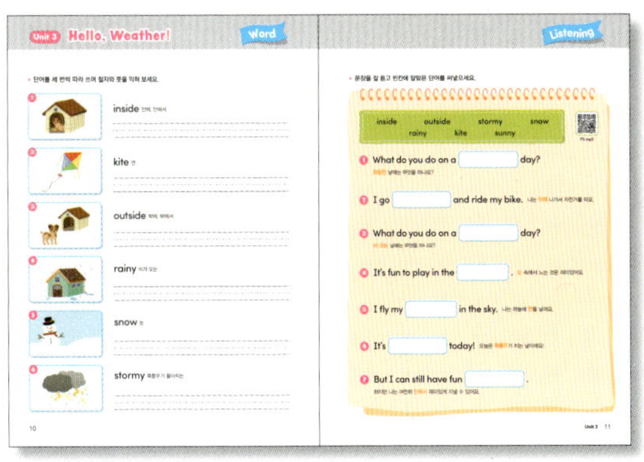

✦ Study Plan ✦

학습 완주를 위해 미리 학습계획을 세워 보세요.
주 5일 학습하여 한 달 완성하기, 또는 주 3일 학습하여 6주 완성하기!
나에게 맞는 계획은 어느 쪽인가요? 목표를 세운 다음, 아래 진도표를 따라 공부해 보세요.

주 5일 학습 스케줄

4 Week

Week 1	Unit 1	Unit 1	Unit 1	Unit 2	Unit 2
	Step 1 읽기 본책 p.12~19 별책 p. 2	Step 2 이해 본책 p. 20~23 별책 p. 3	Step 3 확장 본책 p. 24~26 별책 p. 4~5	Step 1 읽기 본책 p. 28~35 별책 p. 6	Step 2 이해 본책 p. 36~39 별책 p. 7
	◯월◯일	◯월◯일	◯월◯일	◯월◯일	◯월◯일
Week 2	Unit 2	Unit 3	Unit 3	Unit 3	Review Test 1
	Step 3 확장 본책 p. 40~42 별책 p. 8~9	Step 1 읽기 본책 p. 44~51 별책 p.10	Step 2 이해 본책 p. 52~55 별책 p.11	Step 3 확장 본책 p. 56~58 별책 p.12~13	본책 p. 59~62
	◯월◯일	◯월◯일	◯월◯일	◯월◯일	◯월◯일
Week 3	Unit 4	Unit 4	Unit 4	Unit 5	Unit 5
	Step 1 읽기 본책 p. 64~71 별책 p.14	Step 2 이해 본책 p. 72~75 별책 p.15	Step 3 확장 본책 p. 76~78 별책 p.16~17	Step 1 읽기 본책 p. 80~87 별책 p.18	Step 2 이해 본책 p. 88~91 별책 p.19
	◯월◯일	◯월◯일	◯월◯일	◯월◯일	◯월◯일
Week 4	Unit 5	Unit 6	Unit 6	Unit 6	Review Test 2
	Step 3 확장 본책 p. 92~94 별책 p. 20~21	Step 1 읽기 본책 p. 96~103 별책 p. 22	Step 2 이해 본책 p.104~107 별책 p. 23	Step 3 확장 본책 p.108~110 별책 p. 24~25	본책 p.111~114
	◯월◯일	◯월◯일	◯월◯일	◯월◯일	◯월◯일

주 3일 학습 스케줄

6 Week

Week 1 Unit 1	**Step 1** 읽기 본책 p.12~19 별책 p. 2	**Step 2** 이해 본책 p. 20~23 별책 p. 3	**Step 3** 확장 본책 p. 24~26 별책 p. 4~5	
	◯월◯일	◯월◯일	◯월◯일	
Week 2 Unit 2	**Step 1** 읽기 본책 p. 28~35 별책 p. 6	**Step 2** 이해 본책 p. 36~39 별책 p. 7	**Step 3** 확장 본책 p. 40~42 별책 p. 8~9	
	◯월◯일	◯월◯일	◯월◯일	
Week 3 Unit 3	**Step 1** 읽기 본책 p. 44~51 별책 p.10	**Step 2** 이해 본책 p. 52~55 별책 p.11	**Step 3** 확장 본책 p. 56~58 별책 p.12~13	**Review Test 1** 본책 p. 59~62
	◯월◯일	◯월◯일	◯월◯일	◯월◯일
Week 4 Unit 4	**Step 1** 읽기 본책 p. 64~71 별책 p.14	**Step 2** 이해 본책 p. 72~75 별책 p.15	**Step 3** 확장 본책 p. 76~78 별책 p.16~17	
	◯월◯일	◯월◯일	◯월◯일	
Week 5 Unit 5	**Step 1** 읽기 본책 p. 80~87 별책 p.18	**Step 2** 이해 본책 p. 88~91 별책 p.19	**Step 3** 확장 본책 p. 92~94 별책 p. 20~21	
	◯월◯일	◯월◯일	◯월◯일	
Week 6 Unit 6	**Step 1** 읽기 본책 p. 96~103 별책 p. 22	**Step 2** 이해 본책 p.104~107 별책 p. 23	**Step 3** 확장 본책 p.108~110 별책 p. 24~25	**Review Test 2** 본책 p.111~114
	◯월◯일	◯월◯일	◯월◯일	◯월◯일

Read Aloud를 위한 4가지 음원

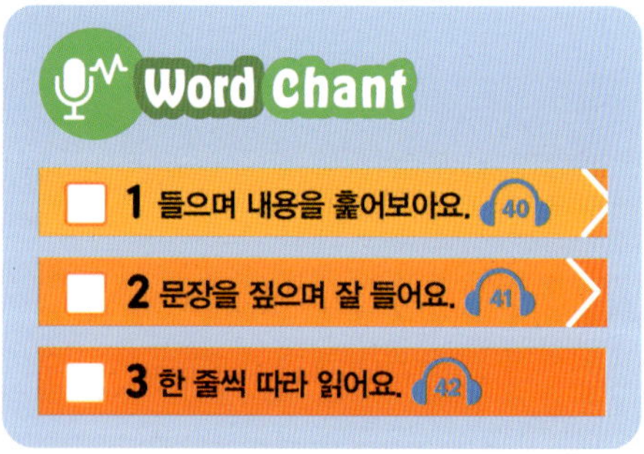

- 읽기 준비를 위한 [단어 챈트]
- 그림과 함께 [스토리 듣기]
- 글자를 짚으며 [집중 듣기]
- 한 문장씩 [따라 읽기]

길벗스쿨 e클래스 에서 오디오 바로 듣기

eclass.gilbut.co.kr에서 학습에 필요한 모든 음원를 제공합니다.
오디오 번호를 찾아 한 번만 탭하면 단어와 스토리를 바로 들을 수 있어요.

학습의 재미를 더하는 스티커 활동!

그림 스티커를 붙이며 단어·문장을 익혀요.

Unit 1

Looking for Max in Town

STEP 1 읽기	STEP 2 이해	STEP 3 확장
핵심 단어를 익혀서 스토리 듣고 읽기	읽은 내용을 점검하며 스토리 이해하기	주제별 필수 어휘를 익혀서 어휘력 강화하기

Key Words

A 그림을 보며 단어를 잘 들어 보세요. 01

town

firefighter

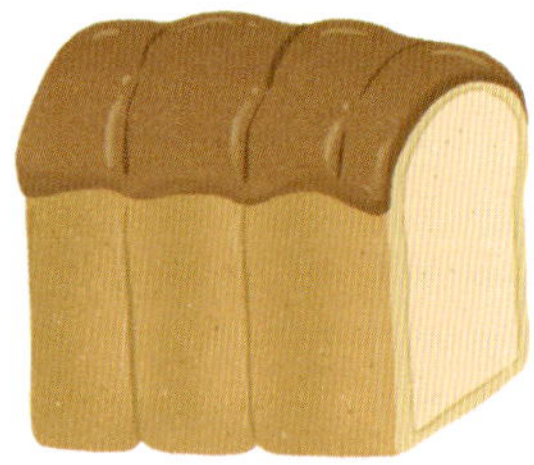

bread

library

police officer

vet

Word Chant

단어를 하나씩 짚으며 단어챈트를 따라 말해 봐요. 02

B 영어 단어와 우리말 뜻을 연결하고, 단어를 따라 쓰세요.

	English		Korean	
1	library		수의사	
2	vet		시내	
3	town		소방관	
4	bread		도서관	
5	firefighter		경찰관	
6	police officer		빵	

Looking for Max in Town

Sam is going to town with his mom.
Max is coming too.

Oh no, Max is missing!

★They go to the fire station.

A firefighter is carrying a fire hose.

They go to the bakery.
A baker is baking bread.

They go to the library.

★They see a librarian there.

★They see ... there. 그들은 거기에서 ~을 봐요

They go to the police station.
They see a police officer there.

They go to the vet clinic.
They see a vet there.

The vet is checking Max.
"He is healthy," says the vet.

Story Check

A 그림에 알맞은 단어를 찾아 동그라미 하세요.

1 

w p o l i c e v e t e b a k e r

2 

m i s s i n g l i b r a r y m w

3 

b a k e r b r e a d f i s h i p

4 

h o s e n t o w n d f u s y o d

B 문장을 잘 듣고, 알맞은 그림에 번호를 쓰세요. 06

C 알맞은 단어에 동그라미 하여 문장을 완성하세요.

1 They (go / miss) to the fire station.

2 A (firefighter / baker) is baking bread.

3 They see a (vet / librarian) there.

Speak & Write! 알맞은 단어를 넣어 문장을 소리 내어 읽은 다음, 써 보세요.

library bakery

They go to the ________. (그들은 ~로 가요.)

baker vet

They see a ________ there. (그들은 거기에서 ~를 봐요.)

D 문장을 읽고, 이야기 순서에 맞는 그림의 기호를 쓰세요.

a

b

c

d

◯ Oh no, Max is missing!

↓

◯ They go to the bakery.

↓

◯ "Have you seen a small dog?" "Yes. I saw one over there."

↓

◯ The vet is checking Max.

엄마와 Sam은 Max를 찾기 위해 어디에 갔나요? 모두 골라 보세요.

☐ police station ☐ fire station ☐ school

E 들으며 빈칸을 채운 다음, 내용에 맞는 그림 스티커를 찾아 붙이세요. 07

1

sticker

They go to the fire station.
A f__________ is carrying a fire hose.
"Have you seen a small dog?"
"No, I haven't."

2

They go to the b__________.
A baker is baking bread.
"Have you seen a small dog?"
"No, I haven't."

3

sticker

They go to the l__________.
They see a librarian there.
"Have you seen a small dog?"
"No, I haven't."

4

sticker

They go to the v__________ clinic.
They see a vet there.
The vet is checking Max.
"He is h__________," says the vet.

library	firefighter	healthy	vet	bakery

Theme Words

Jobs

직업과 관련된 단어들을 잘 듣고, 단어를 따라 쓰세요. 08

❶ teacher

t

❷ nurse

n

❸ police officer

p

❹ bus driver

b

❺ vet

v

❻ baker

b

◆ 우리 주변에는 어떤 일을 하는 사람들이 있나요? 단어를 써 보세요.

제빵사

_ a _ er

경찰관

po _ _ ce o _ _ _ cer

수의사

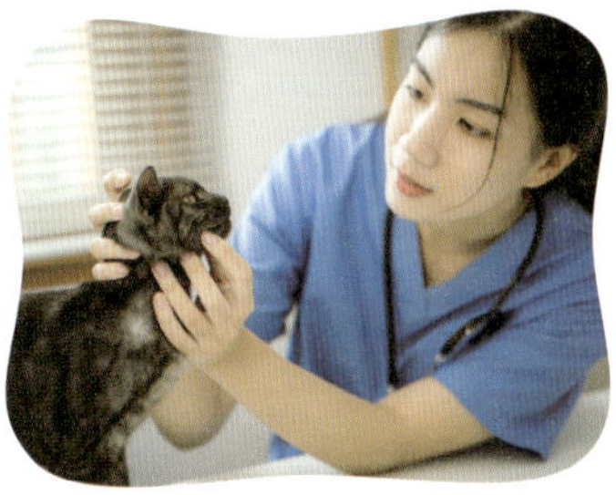

_ e _

버스 운전사

_ _ _ dri _ _ _

간호사

n _ _ se

선생님

tea _ _ _ _

What do you want to be?

여러분은 나중에 무엇이 되고 싶나요?

I want to be a/an ______________________.

Looking for Max in Town

sticker

A firefighter is carrying a fire hose.
"Have you seen a small dog?"
"No, I haven't."

sticker

They see a librarian there.
"Have you seen a small dog?"
"No, I haven't."

sticker

They see a police officer there.
"Have you seen a small dog?"
"Yes. I saw one over there."

sticker

They see a vet there.
The vet is checking Max.
"He is healthy," says the vet.

Self-Check

- ☐ 스티커를 바르게 붙였어요.
- ☐ 주요 단어의 뜻을 잘 알아요.
- ☐ 막힘 없이 술술 읽었어요.

알맞은 문장 스티커를 붙여 글을 완성하고,
큰 소리로 읽어 보세요.
오디오를 들으며 잘 읽었는지 확인해 보세요. 09

Unit 2

Our Special House

읽기
STEP 1
핵심 단어를 익혀서
스토리 듣고 읽기

이해
STEP 2
읽은 내용을 점검하며
스토리 이해하기

확장
STEP 3
주제별 필수 어휘를 익혀서
어휘력 강화하기

Key Words

A 그림을 보며 단어를 잘 들어 보세요. 10

watch

bedroom

kitchen

delicious

bathtub

blanket

Word Chant

단어를 하나씩 짚으며 단어챈트를 따라 말해 봐요. 11

B 영어 단어와 우리말 뜻을 연결하고, 단어를 따라 쓰세요.

	영어	우리말
1	bedroom	담요, 이불
2	kitchen	침실, 방
3	blanket	보다
4	delicious	부엌
5	watch	욕조
6	bathtub	맛있는

Our Special House

Welcome to our house!
We have fun rooms.
Come and see!

★We have a big living room.
My family talks here.

We like to watch movies here.

★We have ... 우리는 (집안의 장소)를 가지고 있어요

We have three bedrooms.
My room has a cool bed.
★I like to dream of space here.

★ I like to ... 나는 ~하는 것을 좋아해요

We have a sunny kitchen.
We cook and eat here.
It always smells so delicious.

We have a small bathroom.
There is a shower and a bathtub.
I like to make bubbles.

We have a special room!

It's Joey's blanket fort.

He likes to play there all day.

Story Check

A 그림에 알맞은 단어를 찾아 동그라미 하세요.

1 

t b l a n k e t v b a t h e d p

2 

b u b b l e n d w a t c h l m e

3 

b e d q b a t h t u b s m e l l

4 

d g s u n n y d e l i c i o u s

B 문장을 잘 듣고, 알맞은 그림에 번호를 쓰세요. 15

C 문장을 읽고 알맞은 그림과 연결하세요.

1 We have a big living room. •

2 We have a small bathroom. •

3 It's Joey's blanket fort. •

• 

• 

• 

Speak & Write! 알맞은 단어를 넣어 문장을 소리 내어 읽은 다음, 써 보세요.

kitchen bathroom

We have a small ________.
(우리는 작은 ~을 가지고 있어요.)

dream cook

I like to ________ here.
(나는 여기서 ~하는 것을 좋아해요.)

D 그림과 문장이 일치하면 True, 일치하지 않으면 False에 동그라미 하세요.

1

We like to watch movies here.

True False

2

Joey likes to cook there all day.

True False

3

We have a sunny bedroom.

True False

4

There is a shower and a bathtub.

True False

주인공의 가족이 함께 모이는 공간은 어디인가요? 모두 고르세요.

☐ kitchen ☐ living room ☐ bathroom

E 들으며 빈칸을 채운 다음, 내용에 맞는 그림 스티커를 찾아 붙이세요. 16

1

sticker

Welcome to our h________ !

We have fun rooms.

Come and see!

2

We have a big l________ .

My family talks here.

We like to w________ movies here.

3

sticker

We have three bedrooms.

My room has a cool b________ .

I like to dream of space here.

4

sticker

We have a special room!

It's Joey's b________ fort.

He likes to play there all day.

bed	house	watch	living room	blanket

Theme Words

Our House

집의 장소와 관련된 단어들을 잘 듣고 따라 쓰세요. 17

① bedroom
b

② laundry room
l

③ bathroom
b

④ living room
l

⑤ stairs
s

⑥ kitchen
k

◆ 집 안에는 어떤 공간들이 있나요? 단어를 써 보세요.

침실, 방

b _ dr _ _ m

욕실

_ _ th _ oo _

거실

_ _ _ ing room

계단

st _ _ _ s

부엌

k _ t _ _ en

세탁실

laun _ _ _ room

What is your favorite room?

여러분이 집에서 가장 좋아하는 공간은 어디인가요?

My favorite room is the ______________.

I Can Read

Our Special House

sticker

My family talks here.
We like to **watch** movies here.

sticker

My room has a cool **bed**.
I like to dream of space here.

sticker

We **cook** and eat here.
It always smells so delicious.

sticker

There is a **shower** and a **bathtub**.
I like to make **bubbles**.

We have a special room!
It's Joey's **blanket** fort.
He likes to play there all day.

Self-Check

- ☐ 스티커를 바르게 붙였어요.
- ☐ 주요 단어의 뜻을 잘 알아요.
- ☐ 막힘 없이 술술 읽었어요.

알맞은 문장 스티커를 붙여 글을 완성하고,
큰 소리로 읽어 보세요.
오디오를 들으며 잘 읽었는지 확인해 보세요. 18

Unit 3

Hello, Weather!

STEP 1 읽기

핵심 단어를 익혀서
스토리 듣고 읽기

STEP 2 이해

읽은 내용을 점검하며
스토리 이해하기

STEP 3 확장

주제별 필수 어휘를 익혀서
어휘력 강화하기

Key Words

A 그림을 보며 단어를 잘 들어 보세요. 19

outside

rainy

snow

kite

stormy

inside

Word Chant

단어를 하나씩 짚으며 단어챈트를 따라 말해 봐요. 20

B 영어 단어와 우리말 뜻을 연결하고, 단어를 따라 쓰세요.

	English	Korean
1	snow	연
2	outside	눈
3	kite	밖에, 밖에서
4	stormy	비가 오는
5	inside	안에, 안에서
6	rainy	폭풍우가 몰아치는

Hello, Weather!

It's sunny today.

★ What do you do on a sunny day?

I go outside and ride my bike.

★ What do you do on a ... day? (날씨가) ~한 날에는 무엇을 하나요?

What do you do on a rainy day?
I go outside and jump in puddles.
★It's fun to play in the rain.

★ It's fun to play ... ~에서 노는 것은 재미있어요

What do you do on a snowy day?
I go outside and make snowballs.
It's fun to play in the snow.

What do you do on a windy day?
I fly my kite in the sky.
It's fun to play outside.

Boom! I hear thunder.
It's stormy today!

I can't go outside on a stormy day.

But I can still have fun inside.
I can read, build, and paint!
Any weather is good for playing.

Story Check

A 그림에 알맞은 단어를 찾아 동그라미 하세요.

1 

z s t o r m y d s u n n y k i t

2 

d r a i n j u m p d s n o w q w

3 

c a t i n t o o u t s i d e s d

4 

b i n s i d e t o u t b a l l r

B 문장을 잘 듣고, 알맞은 그림에 번호를 쓰세요. 24

C 알맞은 단어에 동그라미 하여 문장을 완성하세요.

1

It's (sunny / snowy) today.

2

What do you do on a (rainy / windy) day?

3

I can't go (outside / inside) on a stormy day.

Speak & Write! 알맞은 단어를 넣어 문장을 소리 내어 읽은 다음, 써 보세요.

sunny rainy

What do you do on a ________ day?
(날씨가 ~한 날에는 무엇을 하나요?)

rain snow

It's fun to play in the ________.
(~에서 노는 것은 재미있어요.)

D 그림과 문장이 일치하면 True, 일치하지 않으면 False에 동그라미 하세요.

1

I go outside and jump in puddles.

True False

2

It's fun to play in the rain.

True False

3

I ride my bike on a stormy day.

True False

4

Boom! I hear thunder.

True False

어떤 날씨에 연을 날리기 좋나요?

☐ windy ☐ stormy ☐ rainy ☐ snowy

E 들으며 빈칸을 채운 다음, 내용에 맞는 그림 스티커를 찾아 붙이세요. 25

1

sticker

It's sunny today.
What do you do on a sunny day?
I go o__________ and ride my bike.

2

sticker

What do you do on a snowy day?
I go outside and make snowballs.
It's fun to play in the s__________.

3

sticker

Boom! I hear t__________.
It's stormy today!
I can't go outside on a stormy day.

4

But I can still have fun i__________.
I can read, build, and paint!
Any w__________ is good for playing.

weather	inside	thunder	outside	snow

Theme Words

Weather

날씨와 관련된 단어들을 잘 듣고, 단어를 따라 쓰세요. 26

2 rainy

r

1 sunny

s

3 snowy

s

4 windy

w

5 stormy

s

6 cloudy

c

◆ 날씨를 나타내는 그림을 보고 단어를 써 보세요.

구름이 잔뜩 낀

cl __ __ d __

눈이 내리는

__ __ owy

폭풍우가 몰아치는

st __ __ my

비가 내리는

__ __ __ ny

바람이 부는

wi __ __ y

화창한

__ __ __ ny

What's the weather like today?

오늘의 날씨는 어떤가요?

It's ____________________ today.

I Can Read

Hello, Weather!

sticker

What do you do on a sunny day?
I go outside and ride my **bike**.

What do you do on a **rainy** day?
I go outside and jump in **puddles**.
It's fun to play in the rain.

What do you do on a **snowy** day?
I go outside and make **snowballs**.

sticker

What do you do on a **windy** day?

sticker

It's fun to play outside.

I can't go outside on a **stormy** day.

sticker

I can read, build, and **paint**!

Self-Check

- ☐ 스티커를 바르게 붙였어요.
- ☐ 주요 단어의 뜻을 잘 알아요.
- ☐ 막힘 없이 술술 읽었어요.

알맞은 문장 스티커를 붙여 글을 완성하고,
큰 소리로 읽어 보세요.
오디오를 들으며 잘 읽었는지 확인해 보세요. 27

Review Test ❶

Words 그림에 맞는 단어를 찾아 쓰세요.

/ 10

kitchen	bread	kite	bathtub	inside
vet	outside	blanket	stormy	library

1  ______________

2  ______________

3  ______________

4  ______________

5  ______________

6  ______________

7  ______________

8  ______________

9  ______________

10  ______________

Comprehension A 문장을 읽고 알맞은 그림의 기호를 쓰세요.

/ 6

1 It's fun to play in the rain. ( )

a 

b 

2 A baker is baking bread. ( )

a 

b 

3 There is a shower and a bathtub. ( )

a 

b 

4 We have a sunny kitchen. ( )

5 It's stormy today! ( )

6 A firefighter is carrying a fire hose. ( )

a 

b 

c 

Comprehension B 그림을 보고 알맞은 문장에 V 표시를 하세요.

/ 6

1 

- [ ] It's Joey's blanket fort.
- [ ] It's Joey's kitchen.

2 

- [ ] They go to the police station.
- [ ] They go to the vet clinic.

3 

- [ ] I fly my kite in the sky.
- [ ] I make snowballs.

4 

- [ ] I like to dream of space.
- [ ] I like to dream of snow.

5

- [ ] Do you see a small dog?
- [ ] Have you seen a small dog?

6

- [ ] I go outside and ride my bike.
- [ ] I read, build, and paint.

정답 ▶ 별책 p.40

Theme Words 그림을 보고 알맞은 단어를 빈칸에 쓰세요.

/ 9

Jobs

1 
n______

2 
p______

3 
teacher

4 
b______

Weather

5 
stormy

6 
s______

7 
s______

8 
w______

Our house

9 
k______

10 
stairs

11 
b______

12 
l______

Unit 4

The Yummy Sandwich

STEP 1 읽기
핵심 단어를 익혀서
스토리 듣고 읽기

STEP 2 이해
읽은 내용을 점검하며
스토리 이해하기

STEP 3 확장
주제별 필수 어휘를 익혀서
어휘력 강화하기

Key Words

A 그림을 보며 단어를 잘 들어 보세요. 28

sandwich

slice

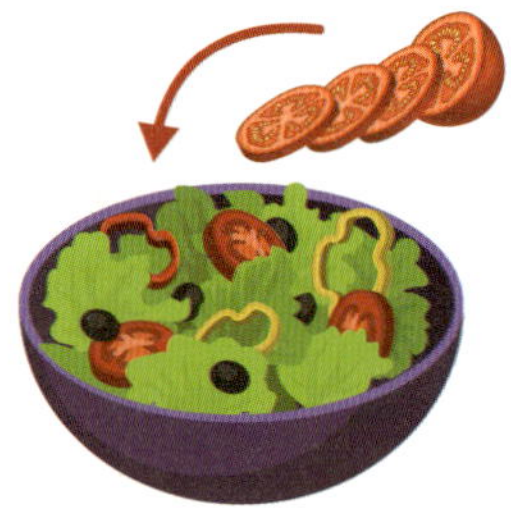

add

spread

half

share

Word Chant

단어를 하나씩 짚으며 단어챈트를 따라 말해 봐요. 29

B 영어 단어와 우리말 뜻을 연결하고, 단어를 따라 쓰세요.

	English	Korean
1	add	나누다, 나눠 먹다
2	slice	더하다
3	sandwich	반, 절반
4	share	(음식을 얇게 썬) 조각
5	spread	샌드위치
6	half	(버터 등을) 바르다

The Yummy Sandwich

Are you hungry?

Let's make a sandwich!

It's easy and fun.

First, toast two slices of bread.

Spread butter on them.

★This makes the sandwich tasty.

★ This makes the sandwich ... 이것은 샌드위치를 ~하게 만들어요

Now, get a slice of cheese.

Put it on the bread.

★Add some lettuce.

This makes the sandwich fresh!

★Add some ... 약간의 ~을 넣으세요

Then, get a slice of ham.

Put it on the lettuce.

Add some tomatoes.

This makes the sandwich juicy!

Take the other slice of bread.

Place it on top.

Press gently and cut it in half.

Your sandwich is ready!
Share it with a friend.

Story Check

A 그림에 알맞은 단어를 찾아 동그라미 하세요.

1

f a l l w h o l e h a l f s e e

2

g h a m t n s l i c e j a m o n

3

k j s h a r e s l i c e i o f f

4

s p r e a d b y l e t t u c e w

B 문장을 잘 듣고, 알맞은 그림에 번호를 쓰세요. 33

C 알맞은 단어에 동그라미 하여 문장을 완성하세요.

1

Take the other slice of (bread / tomato).
Place it on top.

2

Lettuce makes the sandwich (sweet / fresh)!

3

Get a slice of (cheese / ham).
Put it on the lettuce.

Speak & Write! 알맞은 단어를 넣어 문장을 소리 내어 읽은 다음, 써 보세요.

salty juicy

This makes the sandwich ________.
(이것은 샌드위치를 ~하게 만들어요.)

lettuce ham

Add some ________. (약간의 ~을 넣으세요.)

D 그림과 문장이 일치하면 True, 일치하지 않으면 False에 동그라미 하세요.

1

Spread butter on the ham.

True False

2

Add some lettuce.

True False

3

Tomatoes make the sandwich juicy.

True False

4

Cut the pizza in half.

True False

샌드위치 재료로 사용되지 않은 것은 무엇인가요? 모두 골라 보세요.

☐ lettuce ☐ carrot ☐ tomato ☐ onion

E 들으며 빈칸을 채운 다음, 내용에 맞는 그림 스티커를 찾아 붙이세요. 34

1 

Are you hungry?
Let's make a s__________ !
It's easy and fun.

2 sticker

Now, get a slice of cheese.
Put it on the b__________ .

3 sticker

Add some lettuce.
This makes the sandwich f__________ !

4 

Take the other s__________ of bread.
Place it on top.

5 sticker

Your sandwich is ready!
S__________ it with a friend.

share	sandwich	bread	slice	fresh

Theme Words

Sandwich

샌드위치 재료들의 이름을 잘 듣고, 단어를 따라 쓰세요. 35

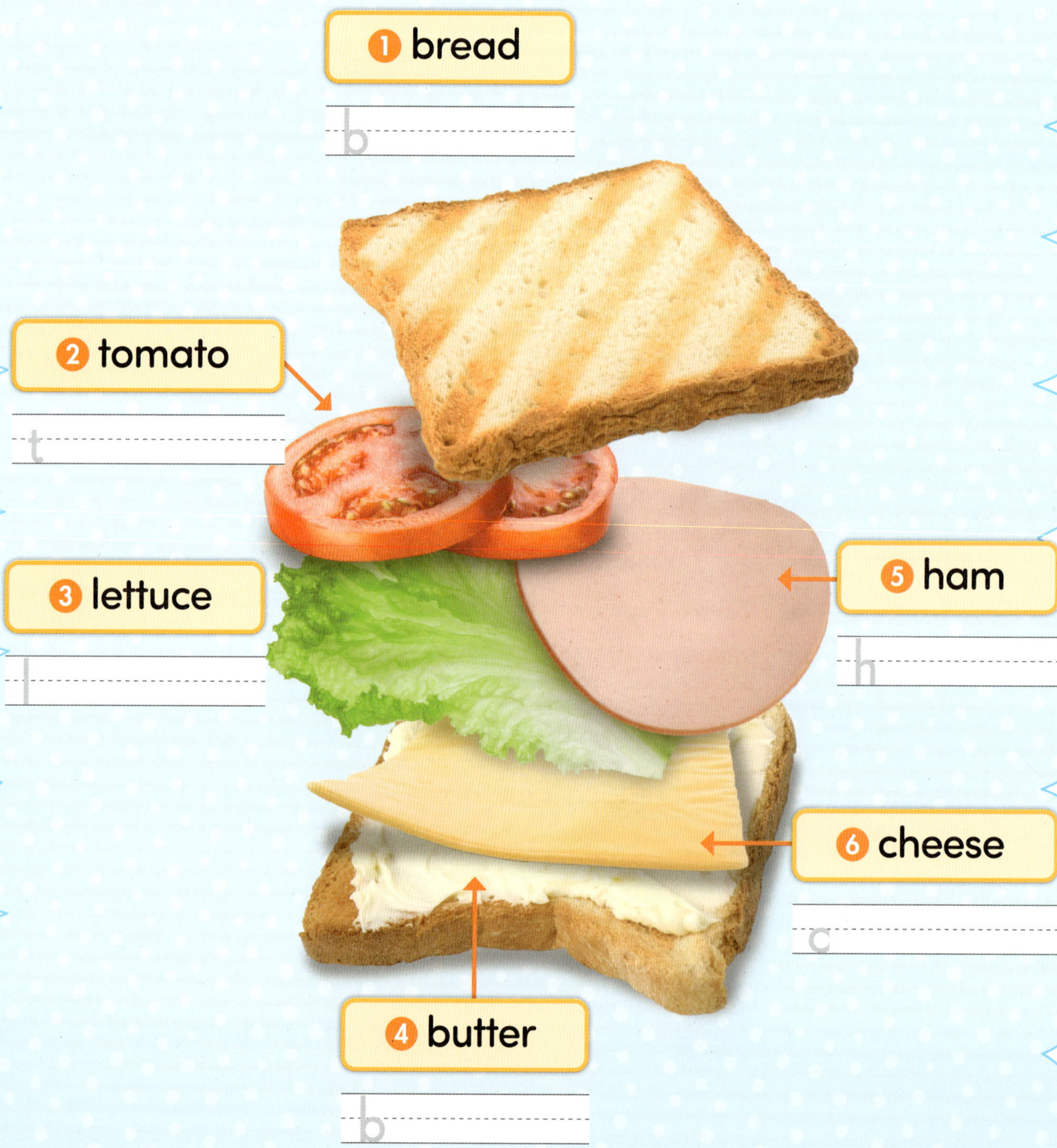

◆샌드위치 재료들의 이름을 써 보세요.

버터

bu _ _ _ _

빵

_ _ ead

치즈

ch _ _ s _

햄

_ a _

토마토

t _ m _ t _

상추

_ _ ttu _ _

What do you like in your sandwich?

여러분이 좋아하는 샌드위치 재료는 무엇인가요?

I like ________, ________, and ________.

I Can Read

The Yummy Sandwich

sticker

Spread **butter** on them.
This makes the sandwich tasty.

Now, get a slice of **cheese**.

sticker

Add some **lettuce**.
This makes the sandwich fresh!

Then, get a slice of **ham**.
Put it on the lettuce.

sticker

This makes the sandwich juicy!

Take the other slice of **bread**.
Place it on top.

sticker

알맞은 문장 스티커를 붙여 글을 완성하고,
큰 소리로 읽어 보세요.
오디오를 들으며 잘 읽었는지 확인해 보세요. 36

Self-Check

- ☐ 스티커를 바르게 붙였어요.
- ☐ 주요 단어의 뜻을 잘 알아요.
- ☐ 막힘 없이 술술 읽었어요.

Unit 5

Robots Everywhere

읽기	이해	확장
STEP 1	STEP 2	STEP 3
핵심 단어를 익혀서 스토리 듣고 읽기	읽은 내용을 점검하며 스토리 이해하기	주제별 필수 어휘를 익혀서 어휘력 강화하기

Key Words

A 그림을 보며 단어를 잘 들어 보세요. 37

clean

patient

order

factory

meal

pick

Word Chant

단어를 하나씩 짚으며 단어챈트를 따라 말해 봐요. 38

B 영어 단어와 우리말 뜻을 연결하고, 단어를 따라 쓰세요.

	English	Korean
1	pick	식사
2	meal	주문, 주문하다
3	patient	(과일 등을) 따다
4	clean	환자
5	order	공장
6	factory	닦다, 청소하다

Robots Everywhere

Robots are everywhere today!
They do many things for us.

Khalif, a Food Delivery Robot in LA

Pepper, a Waiter Robot in Tokyo

A Farming Drone Robot

A Coffee-Making Robot Arm

At Home

Robots can clean the house.

★Can they play with kids?

Yes, they can!

★Can they ...? 그들은 ~을 할 수 있나요?

In a Hospital

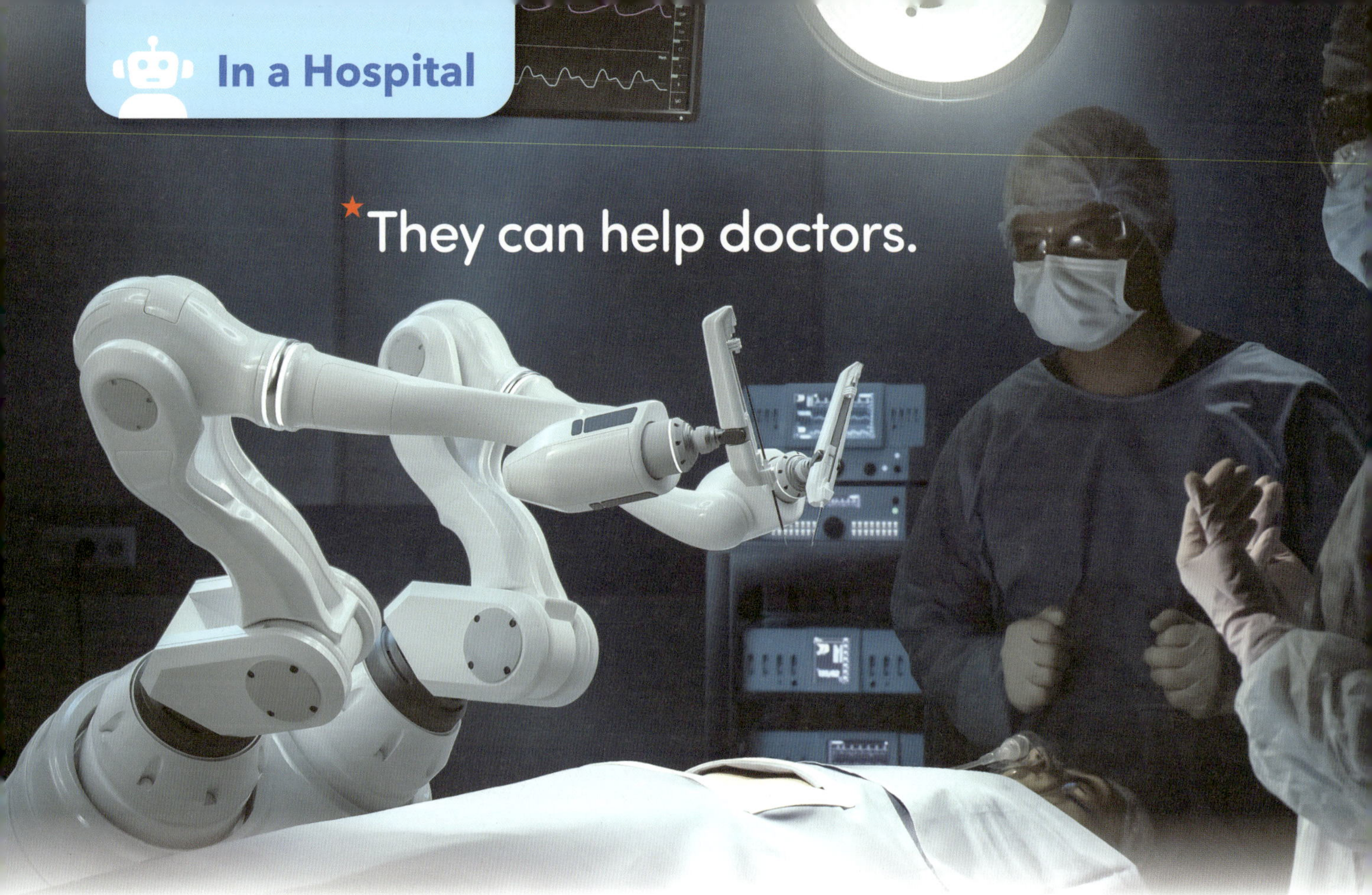

★They can help doctors.

Can they help patients, too?
Yes, they can.

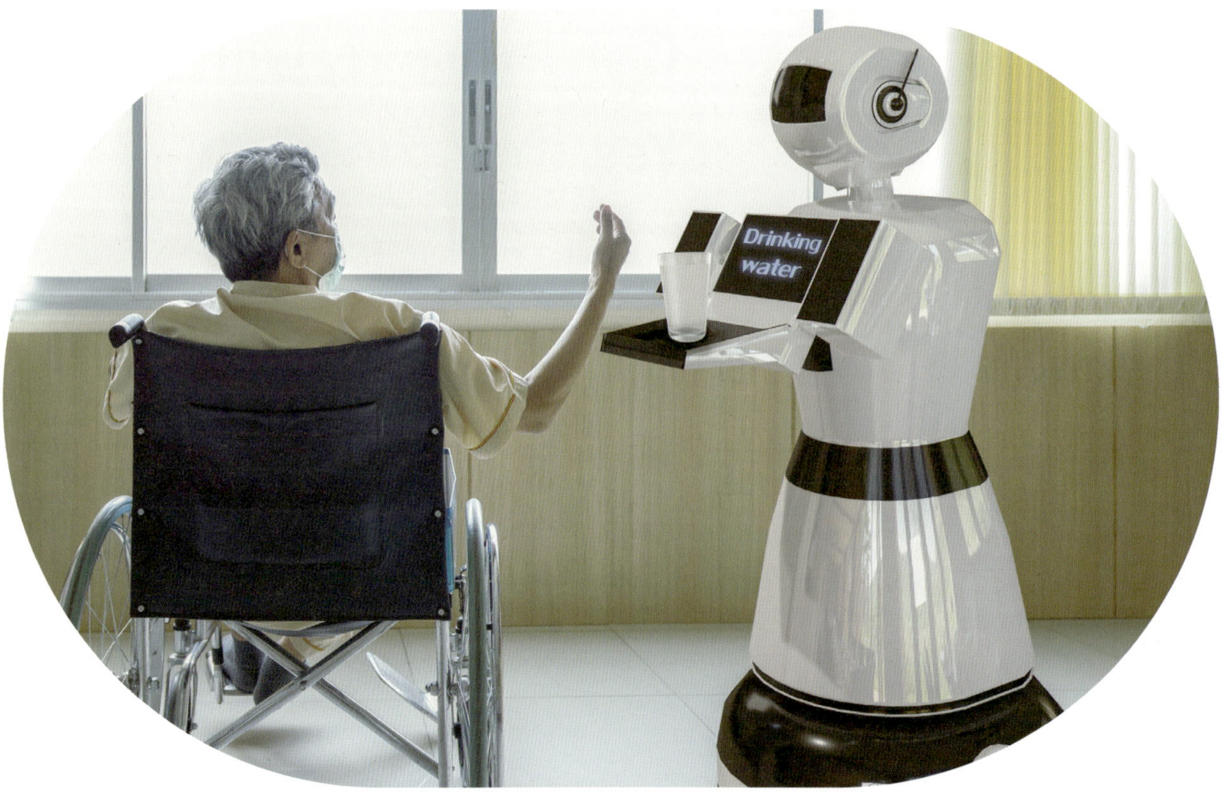

★They can ... 그들은 ~할 수 있어요

Many robot arms work quickly.

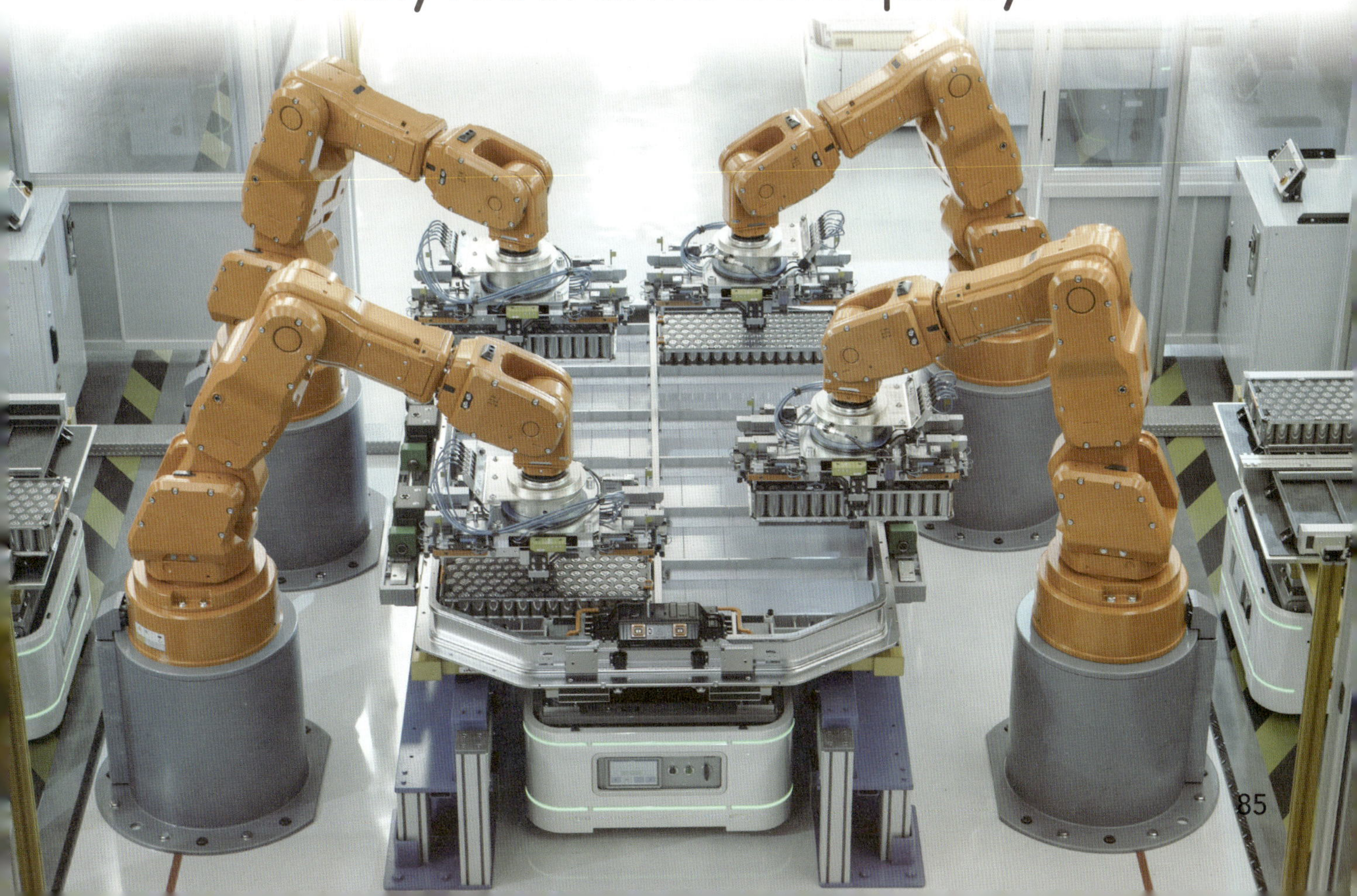

In a Restaurant

Robots can take orders.

They can bring your food, too.

They can also water plants.

Story Check

A 그림에 알맞은 단어를 찾아 동그라미 하세요.

1 

j l m e a l i r c l e a n q o g

2 

z i p i c k y s f l y a r d w l

3 

i d m e a l h o s p i t a l k t

4 

l b i r d s u m e f a c t o r y

B 문장을 잘 듣고, 알맞은 그림에 번호를 쓰세요. 42

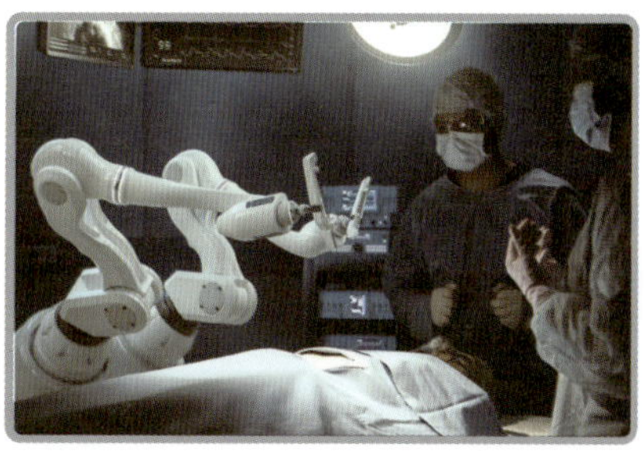

C 문장을 읽고 알맞은 그림과 연결하세요.

1 Robots can pick fruits. •

2 Can they play with kids?
Yes, they can! •

3 Robots can take orders. •

• 

• 

• 

Speak & Write! 알맞은 단어를 넣어 문장을 소리 내어 읽은 다음, 써 보세요.

build cars
pick fruits

They can ________. (그들은 ~할 수 있어요.)

____

doctors patients

Can they help ________?
(그들은 ~을 도울 수 있나요?)

____

D 그림과 문장이 일치하면 True, 일치하지 않으면 False에 동그라미 하세요.

1

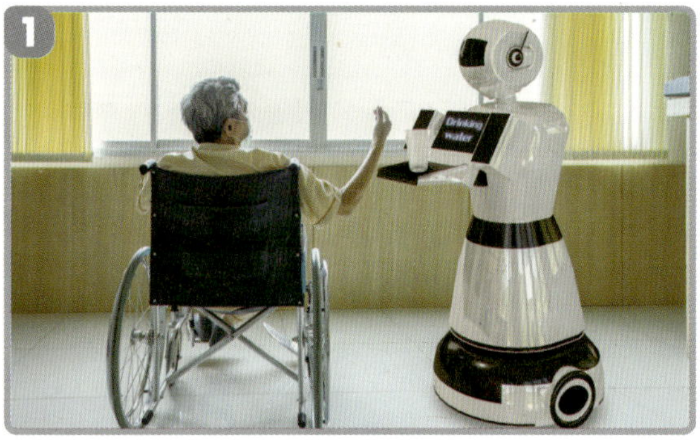

Robots can help patients in a hospital.

True False

2

Robots can't bring your food.

True False

3

Robot arms work slowly in a factory.

True False

4

Robots can cook fruits on a farm.

True False

로봇은 병원에서 누구를 도와줄 수 있나요? 모두 고르세요.

☐ doctors ☐ firefighters ☐ patients ☐ farmers

E 들으며 빈칸을 채운 다음, 내용에 맞는 그림 스티커를 찾아 붙이세요. 43

1

At Home

Robots can c________ the house.

Can they play with kids?

Yes, they can!

2

sticker

In a Hospital

They can help d________.

Can they help patients, too?

Yes, they can.

3

sticker

In a F________

Robots can build cars.

Many robot arms work quickly.

4

sticker

On a Farm

Robots can p________ fruits.

They can also w________ plants.

water	pick	factory	doctors	clean

Theme Words

Places

마을의 장소와 관련된 단어들을 잘 듣고, 단어를 따라 쓰세요. 44

❶ restaurant

r

❷ house

h

❸ factory

f

❹ hospital

h

❺ school

s

❻ bank

b

◆ 다음 사람들이 있는 장소는 어디일까요? 단어를 써 보세요.

집

h __ __ se

식당

res __ __ __ rant

병원

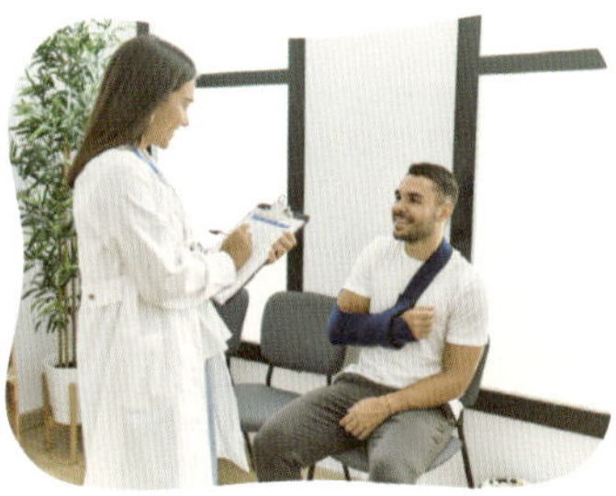

__ __ spi __ __ __

은행

ba __ __

학교

sc __ __ __ __

공장

__ __ __ tory

Have you seen a robot working?

일하는 로봇을 만나본 적 있나요? 그 로봇은 어디에서 일하나요?

The robot works at a ______________________.

I Can Read

Robots Everywhere

At Home

sticker

Can they play with kids?

Yes, they can!

In a Hospital

sticker

Can they help **patients**, too?

Yes, they can.

In a Factory

sticker

Many robot arms work quickly.

In a Restaurant

sticker

They can bring your **food**, too.

알맞은 문장 스티커를 붙여 글을 완성하고,
큰 소리로 읽어 보세요.
오디오를 들으며 잘 읽었는지 확인해 보세요. 45

Self-Check

- ☐ 스티커를 바르게 붙였어요.
- ☐ 주요 단어의 뜻을 잘 알아요.
- ☐ 막힘 없이 술술 읽었어요.

Unit 6

Beaky, the Little Red Hen

STEP 1 읽기
핵심 단어를 익혀서
스토리 듣고 읽기

STEP 2 이해
읽은 내용을 점검하며
스토리 이해하기

STEP 3 확장
주제별 필수 어휘를 익혀서
어휘력 강화하기

Key Words

A 그림을 보며 단어를 잘 들어 보세요. 46

hen

plant

wheat

grow

flour

grind

Word Chant

단어를 하나씩 짚으며 단어챈트를 따라 말해 봐요. 47

B 영어 단어와 우리말 뜻을 연결하고, 단어를 따라 쓰세요.

	English	Korean
1	grow	(곡식 등을) 갈다, 빻다
2	grind	(씨앗 등을) 심다
3	hen	밀가루
4	plant	(식물이) 자라다
5	flour	암탉
6	wheat	밀

Beaky, the Little Red Hen

Beaky, the little red hen,
wants to plant seeds.

The wheat grows tall.

Nobody helps her.
She works all by herself.

★ I'm going to ... 나는 ~할 거예요

The wheat is ready to grind.

★Who will help me ...? 내가 ~하는 것을 누가 도와줄래?

Now Beaky has some flour.

Again, nobody helps her.

She works all by herself.

The bread is ready.
It smells fresh and delicious.

No, you will not.
I'm going to eat it all by myself!

She enjoys the bread.

Story Check

A 그림에 알맞은 단어를 찾아 동그라미 하세요.

1 

t d w h e a t w h e l p w h e a

2 

h b r e a d z g r i n d w m a k

3 

f l o w e r t h o p e f l o u r

4 

f p i g d c a t s i h e n y e d

B 문장을 잘 듣고, 알맞은 그림에 번호를 쓰세요. 51

C 문장을 읽고 알맞은 그림과 연결하세요.

1 "I'm going to harvest the wheat." •

2 "I'm going to eat it all by myself!" •

3 "Who will help me?" "Not me. Oink, oink!" •

• 

• 

• 

Speak & Write! 알맞은 단어를 넣어 문장을 소리 내어 읽은 다음, 써 보세요.

bake plant

Who will help me ________ the bread?
(내가 빵을 ~하는 것을 누가 도와줄래?)

eat harvest

I'm going to ________ the wheat.
(나는 밀을 ~할 거야.)

D 문장을 읽고, 이야기 순서에 맞는 그림의 기호를 쓰세요.

a

b

c

d

○ Beaky, the little red hen, wants to plant seeds.

↓

○ "Who will help me grind the wheat?"

↓

○ The bread is ready. It smells fresh and delicious.

↓

○ "I'm going to eat it all by myself!"

Beaky가 도와달라고 했을 때, 돼지와 고양이가 거절하지 않은 일은 무엇인가요?

☐ plant seeds ☐ bake the bread ☐ eat the bread

E 들으며 빈칸을 채운 다음, 내용에 맞는 그림 스티커를 찾아 붙이세요. 52

1

sticker

The wheat grows tall.
"I'm going to harvest the w______.
Who will h______ me?"
Nobody helps her.

2

Now Beaky has some flour.
"Who will help me bake the b______?"
Again, nobody helps her.
She works all by herself.

3

sticker

The bread is ready.
It smells f______ and delicious.
"Who will help me eat this bread?"
"I will! Oink, oink."

4

sticker

"No, you will not.
I'm going to eat it all by m______!"
She enjoys the bread.

help	wheat	fresh	bread	myself

Theme Words

From Seeds to Bread

밀 씨가 빵이 되는 과정을 살펴보고, 단어를 잘 듣고 따라 쓰세요. 53

1 seeds

2 plant

3 wheat

4 harvest

5 grind

6 flour

7 bake

8 bread

◆ 씨앗이 빵이 되기까지 빨간 암탉은 어떤 일을 했나요? 단어를 써 보세요.

씨앗들

s ☐ ☐ ds

(씨앗 등을) 심다

pla ☐ ☐

밀

☐ ☐ eat

수확하다

har ☐ ☐ ☐ ☐

(곡식 등을) 갈다, 빻다

gri ☐ ☐

(빵 등을) 굽다

b ☐ k ☐

What do we need to make bread?

빵을 만드는 데 필요한 재료는 무엇일까요?

We need ______________ and ______________.

I Can Read

Beaky, the Little Red Hen

sticker

"I'm going to harvest the wheat. Who will help me?"

Nobody helps her.

She works all by herself.

sticker

"Who will help me bake the **bread** ?"

Again, nobody helps her.

She works all by herself.

The **bread** is ready.

"Who will help me eat this bread?"

"I will! Oink, oink."

"I will! Meow, meow."

sticker

I'm going to eat it all by myself!"

She **enjoys** the bread.

Self-Check

- ☐ 스티커를 바르게 붙였어요.
- ☐ 주요 단어의 뜻을 잘 알아요.
- ☐ 막힘 없이 술술 읽었어요.

알맞은 문장 스티커를 붙여 글을 완성하고,
큰 소리로 읽어 보세요.
오디오를 들으며 잘 읽었는지 확인해 보세요. 54

Review Test 2

Words 그림에 맞는 단어를 찾아 쓰세요. / 10

add spread flour order half
factory wheat sandwich patient hen

1  ____________

2  ____________

3  ____________

4  ____________

5  ____________

6  ____________

7  ____________

8  ____________

9  ____________

10 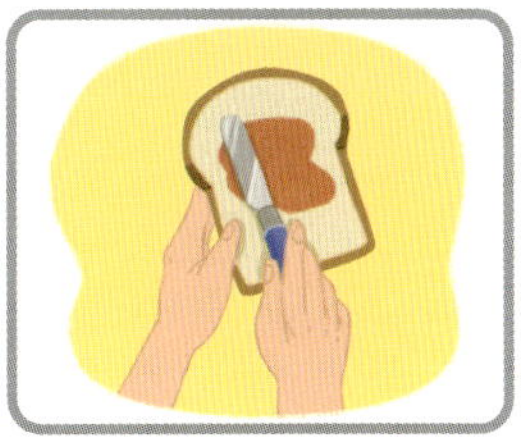 ____________

Comprehension A 문장을 읽고 알맞은 그림의 기호를 쓰세요.

/ 6

1 Robots can pick fruits. ◯

a

b

2 Beaky works all by herself. ◯

a

b

3 Spread butter on them. ◯

a

b

4 Press gently and cut it in half. ◯

5 Beaky wants to plant seeds. ◯

6 Robots can help patients. ◯

a
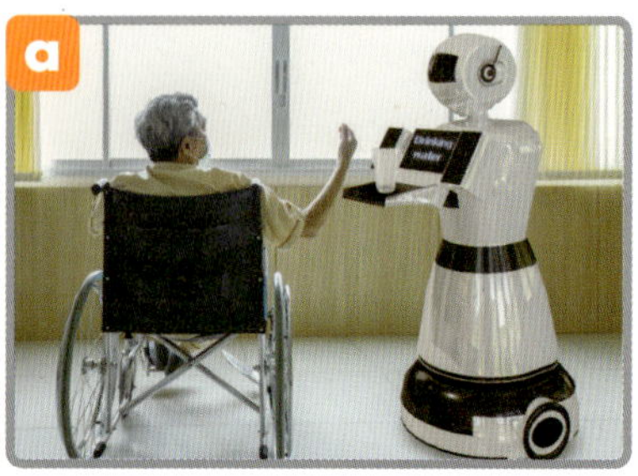

b

c

Comprehension B 그림을 보고 알맞은 문장에 V 표시를 하세요.

/ 6

1

- [ ] She enjoys the bread all by herself.
- [ ] She shares the bread with friends.

2

- [ ] In a hospital, robots can help doctors.
- [ ] In a factory, robots can build cars.

3

- [ ] Add some lettuce.
- [ ] Add some tomatoes.

4

- [ ] Place the other slice of bread on top.
- [ ] Place a slice of cheese on top.

5
- [ ] Who will help me eat this bread?
- [ ] Who will help me harvest the wheat?

6
- [ ] Robots can bring my food.
- [ ] Robots can clean my house.

정답 ▶ 별책 p.40

Theme Words 그림을 보고 알맞은 단어를 빈칸에 쓰세요.

/ 9

From Seeds to Bread

1 

w ______

2 

s ______

3 

b ______

4 

flour

Places

5 

f ______

6 

house

7 

h ______

8 

s ______

Sandwich

9 

c ______

10 

h ______

11 

butter

12 

t ______

SUPER
GOOD!

저자 C2 Archive (대표 Olene Kim)

지난 20여 년간 영어라는 언어를 어린이들이 어려움 없이 단계적으로 습득해갈 수 있도록 효과적인 교수법을 연구하여 다양한 교재로 구현해 온 영어교육 전문 집필진입니다. 파닉스, 리딩, 코스북, 문법 등 여러 분야의 ELT 교재와 영어 단행본 학습서를 집필·개발하였습니다.

저자 기적학습연구소

"혼자서 작은 산을 넘는 아이가 나중에 큰 산도 넘습니다." 본 연구소는 아이들이 혼자서 큰 산까지 넘을 수 있는 힘을 키워주고자 합니다. 아이들의 연령에 맞게 학습의 산을 작게 만들어 혼자서도 쉽게 넘을 수 있게 만듭니다. 때로는 작은 고난도 경험하게 하여 성취감도 맛보게 합니다. 그리고 아이들에게 실제로 적용해서 검증을 통해 차근차근 책을 만듭니다.

기적의 영어리딩 Level 2C

Miracle Series – Reading English

초판 1쇄 인쇄 • 2025년 11월 15일

지은이 • C2 Archive, 기적학습연구소

발행인 • 이종원
발행처 • (주)길벗스쿨
출판사 등록일 • 2025년 5월 28일 | **주소** • 서울시 마포구 월드컵로 10길 56(서교동) | **대표 전화** • 02)332-0931 | **팩스** • 02)323-0586
홈페이지 • www.gilbutschool.co.kr | **이메일** • gilbut@gilbut.co.kr

담당편집 • 이경희(natura@gilbut.co.kr), 최주연, 김예지, 유서현 | **기획** • 이경희, 김남희, 박민혜 | **영문 감수** • Ryan P. Lagace | **디자인** • 이현숙 | **제작** • 손일순
영업마케팅 • 문세연, 박선경, 구혜지, 박다슬 | **웹마케팅** • 박달님, 이재윤, 이지수, 나혜연 | **영업관리** • 정경화 | **독자지원** • 윤정아
전산편집 • 연디자인 | **삽화** • 백정석, 김경주, 박소현, 윤지현, 유정연, 이나영 | **인쇄** • 영림인쇄 | **제본** • 영림제본 | **녹음** • 아람 멀티미디어

Photo Credits
해당 이미지는 Shutterstock.com의 라이선스 하에 사용되었습니다.
p.23 (Hryshchyshen Serhii, PeopleImages, Lee Charlie, Drazen Zigic, Summit Art Creations, aslysun) p.38 (Milena Moiola) p.39 (bluedog studio, Rawpixel.com, Pixel-Shot, Tatiana Diuvbanova, Inna_Kandybka, New Africa) p.54 (Soloviova Liudmyla, Olena Yakobchuk, Yuriy Brykaylo, Olga_Kuzmina,dangrasan9, jean schweitzer) p.80 (Walter Cicchetti, Ned Snowman,NovitaSari Image, asharkyu) p.81 (Pixel-Shot. goodmoments) p.82 (Gorodenkoff, PaO_STUDIO) p.83 (Phonlamai Photo, IM Imagery) p.84 (Zapp2Photo, Raonphoto) p.85 (Scharfsinn, Es sarawuth) p.90 (JRomero04, Photos By The Owl, Vova Shevchuk, Spiroview Inc, Pixel-Shot, Jonathan Weiss) p.91 (fizkes, Ann Kosolapova. Krakenimages.com, New Africa, Rido, thanun vongsuravanich)

ISBN 979-11-7467-049-6 64740 (길벗 도서번호 30616)
정가 17,000원

제 품 명 : 기적의 영어리딩 2C
제조사명 : 길벗스쿨
제조국명 : 대한민국
전화번호 : 02-332-0931
주 소 : 서울시 마포구 월드컵로 10길 56 (서교동)
제조년월 : 판권에 별도 표기
사용연령 : **8세 이상**
KC마크는 이 제품이 공통안전기준에 적합하였음을 의미합니다.

기적 영어 학습서

기본이 탄탄! 실전에서 척척!
유초등 필수 영어능력을 길러주는 코어 학습서

유아 영어

재미있는 액티비티가 가득한
4~6세를 위한 영어 워크북

4세 이상

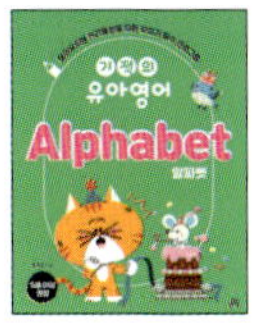

5세 이상

6세 이상

6세 이상

파닉스 완성 프로그램

알파벳 음가 ➜ 사이트워드
➜ 읽기 연습까지!
리딩을 위한 탄탄한 기초 만들기

6세 이상 전 3권

1~3학년

1~3학년 전 3권

영어 단어

영어 실력의 가장 큰 바탕은 어휘력!
교과과정 필수 어휘 익히기

3학년 이상 전 2권

1~2학년 전 2권

3~4학년 전 2권

5~6학년 전 2권

영어 리딩

패턴 문장 리딩으로 시작해
정확한 해석을 위한 끊어 읽기까지!
탄탄한 독해 실력 쌓기

2~3학년 전 3권

3~4학년 전 3권

4~5학년 전 2권

5~6학년 전 2권

5~6학년 전 2권

영어 라이팅

저학년은 패턴 영작으로,
고학년은 5형식 문장 만들기 연습으로
튼튼한 영작 실력 완성

2학년 이상 전 4권

4학년 이상 전 5권

5학년 이상 전 2권

6학년 이상

영어일기

한 줄 쓰기부터 생활일기,
주제일기까지!
영어 글쓰기 실력을 키우는 시리즈

3학년 이상

4~5학년

5~6학년

영문법

중학 영어 대비, 영어 구사
정확성을 키워주는 영문법 학습

4~5학년 전 2권

5~6학년 전 3권

6학년 이상

초등 필수 영어 무작정 따라하기

초등 시기에 놓쳐서는 안 될 필수 학습은 바로 영어 교과서!
영어 교과서 5종의 핵심 내용을 쏙쏙 뽑아 한 권으로 압축 정리했습니다.
초등 과정의 필수학습으로 기초를 다져서 중학교 및 상위 학습의 단단한 토대가 되게 합니다.

1~2학년

2~3학년

2~3학년

3학년 이상

4학년 이상

미국교과서 리딩

문제의 차이가 영어 실력의 차이! 논픽션 리딩에 강해지는 《미국교과서 READING》
논픽션 리딩에 가장 좋은 재료인 미국 교과과정의 주제를 담은 지문을 읽고, 독해력과
문제 해결력을 두루 향상시킬 수 있도록 구성한 단계별 리딩 프로그램

LEVEL 1
준비 단계

LEVEL 2
시작 단계

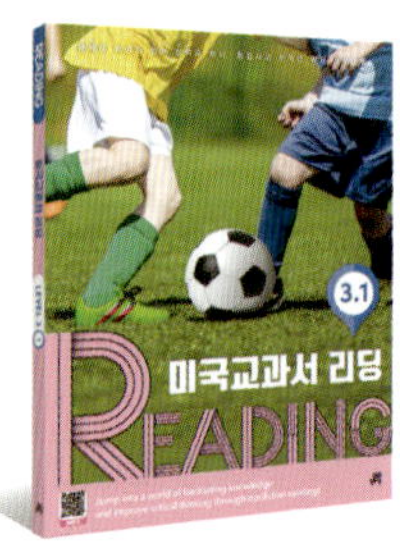

LEVEL 3
정독 연습 단계

LEVEL 4
독해 정확성 향상 단계

LEVEL 5
독해 통합심화 단계

2C

짧은 문장 읽기
AR 0.7~1.5

기적의 영어리딩

with 주제 어휘

Practice Book

(정답과 해석 포함)

길벗스쿨

기적의 영어리딩 2C

Practice Book

(정답과 해석 포함)

▸ 단어를 세 번씩 따라 쓰며 철자와 뜻을 익혀 보세요.

1

bread 빵

2

firefighter 소방관

3

library 도서관

4

police officer 경찰관

5

town 시내

6

vet 수의사

▸ 문장을 잘 듣고 빈칸에 알맞은 단어를 써넣으세요.

town	small	bread	check
vet	fire station	library	

P1.mp3

1. Sam is going to ______ with his mom.
   샘은 엄마와 함께 시내에 가고 있어요.

2. They go to the ______. 그들은 소방서로 가요.

3. A baker is baking ______. 제빵사가 빵을 굽고 있어요.

4. They go to the ______. 그들은 도서관으로 가요.

5. Have you seen a ______ dog? 작은 개를 보셨나요?

6. They see a ______ there. 그들은 거기에서 수의사를 봐요.

7. The vet is ______ing Max. 수의사가 맥스를 살피고 있어요.

▸ 알맞은 단어에 동그라미 한 다음, 전체 문장을 따라 쓰세요.

1 Oh no, Max is (coming / missing)! 오 안돼, 맥스가 없어졌어요!

2 A (librarian / firefighter) is carrying a fire hose. 소방관이 소방호스를 들고 있어요.

3 They go to the (bakery / police station). 그들은 빵집으로 가요.

4 They go to the (police station / fire station). 그들은 경찰서로 가요.

5 They go to the (cat / vet) clinic. 그들은 동물병원에 가요.

6 "He is (healthy / sick)," says the vet. "그는 건강해요." 수의사가 말해요.

Jobs ▸ 그림에 알맞은 단어에 동그라미 한 다음, 단어를 따라 쓰세요.

1

teacher baker

2

vet nurse

3

baker police officer

4

bus driver baker

5

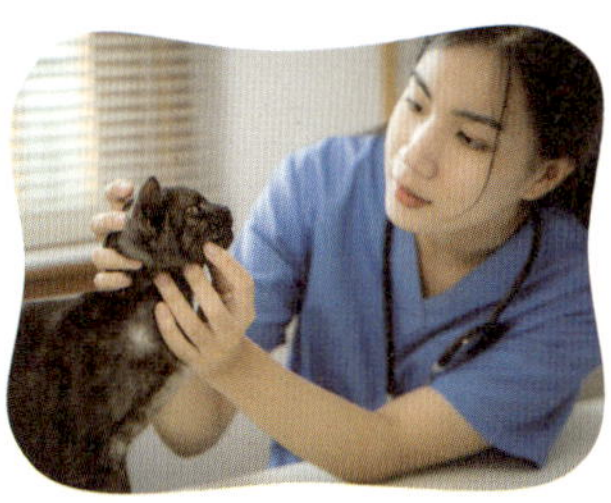

teacher vet

6

baker nurse

▸ 단어를 세 번씩 따라 쓰며 철자와 뜻을 익혀 보세요.

1 

bathtub 욕조

2 

bedroom 침실, 방

3 

blanket 담요, 이불

4 

delicious 맛있는

5 

kitchen 부엌

6 

watch 보다

Listening

▸ 문장을 잘 듣고 빈칸에 알맞은 단어를 써넣으세요.

living room　　special　　blanket　　bathtub
bed　　kitchen　　bubble

P2.mp3

1 We have a big ________ . 우리는 큰 거실을 가지고 있어요.

2 My room has a cool ________ . 내 방에는 멋진 침대가 있어요.

3 We have a sunny ________ . 우리는 햇빛이 환한 부엌을 가지고 있어요.

4 There is a shower and a ________ .
거기엔 샤워기와 욕조가 있어요.

5 I like to make ________ s. 나는 거품을 만드는 것을 좋아해요.

6 We have a ________ room! 우리는 특별한 방을 가지고 있어요!

7 It's Joey's ________ fort. 그건 조이의 담요 요새예요.

▸ 알맞은 단어에 동그라미 한 다음, 전체 문장을 따라 쓰세요.

1. We like to (watch / see) movies here. 우리는 여기서 영화 보는 것을 좋아해요.

2. We have three (kitchens / bedrooms). 우리는 침실 세 개를 가지고 있어요.

3. We (cook / sleep) and eat here. 우리는 여기서 요리하고 식사해요.

4. It always smells so (bad / delicious). 그곳에선 항상 매우 맛있는 냄새가 나요.

5. We have a small (bathroom / bedroom). 우리는 작은 욕실을 가지고 있어요.

6. He likes to (play /make) there all day. 그는 하루 종일 거기서 노는 것을 좋아해요.

Our House ▸ 사람들이 있는 공간에 동그라미 한 다음, 단어를 따라 쓰세요.

1

bathroom bedroom

2

laundry room stairs

3

kitchen bathroom

4

bedroom living room

5

stairs laundry room

6

bathroom kitchen

▸ 단어를 세 번씩 따라 쓰며 철자와 뜻을 익혀 보세요.

1

inside 안에, 안에서

2
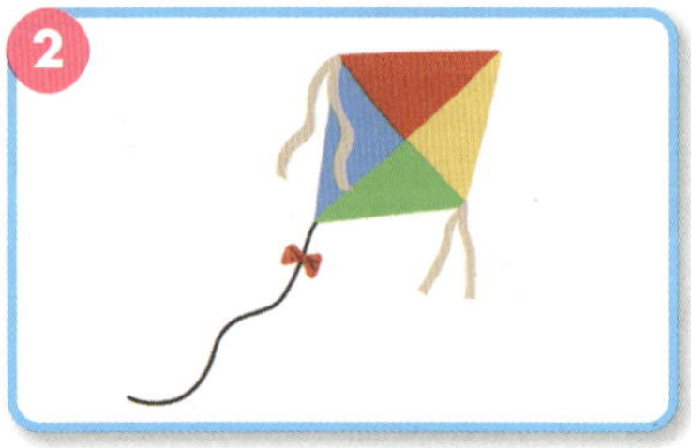

kite 연

3

outside 밖에, 밖에서

4

rainy 비가 오는

5

snow 눈

6

stormy 폭풍우가 몰아치는

▸ 문장을 잘 듣고 빈칸에 알맞은 단어를 써넣으세요.

inside	outside	stormy	snow
rainy	kite	sunny	

P3.mp3

1. What do you do on a ________ day?
화창한 날에는 무엇을 하나요?

2. I go ________ and ride my bike. 나는 밖에 나가서 자전거를 타요.

3. What do you do on a ________ day?
비 오는 날에는 무엇을 하나요?

4. It's fun to play in the ________ . 눈 속에서 노는 것은 재미있어요.

5. I fly my ________ in the sky. 나는 하늘에 연을 날려요.

6. It's ________ today! 오늘은 폭풍우가 치는 날이에요!

7. But I can still have fun ________ .
하지만 나는 여전히 안에서 재미있게 지낼 수 있어요.

▸ 알맞은 단어에 동그라미 한 다음, 전체 문장을 따라 쓰세요.

1. It's (sunny / stormy) today. 오늘은 화창한 날이에요.

2. I go (inside / outside) and jump in puddles.
나는 밖에 나가서 물웅덩이에 뛰어들어요.

3. What do you do on a (snowy / rainy) day? 눈 오는 날에는 무엇을 하나요?

4. What do you do on a (windy / sunny) day? 바람 부는 날에는 무엇을 하나요?

5. I hear (storm / thunder). 나는 천둥 소리가 들려요.

6. Any (weather / place) is good for playing. 어떤 날씨든 놀기 좋아요.

Weather ▸ 그림에 알맞은 단어에 동그라미 한 다음, 단어를 따라 쓰세요.

1

cloudy sunny

2

rainy stormy

3

snowy windy

4

windy cloudy

5

sunny stormy

6

snowy cloudy

Unit 4 The Yummy Sandwich

Word

▸ 단어를 세 번씩 따라 쓰며 철자와 뜻을 익혀 보세요.

1

add 더하다

2

half 반, 절반

3

sandwich 샌드위치

4

share 나누다, 나눠 먹다

5

slice (음식을 얇게 썬) 조각

6
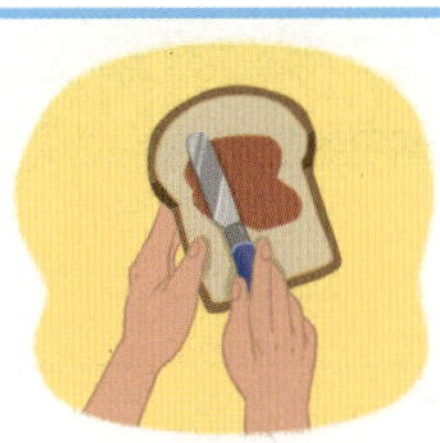

spread (버터 등을) 바르다

▸ 문장을 잘 듣고 빈칸에 알맞은 단어를 써넣으세요.

butter	slice	sandwich	share
bread	lettuce	fresh	

P4.mp3

1. Let's make a ______ ! 샌드위치를 만들어 보자!

2. First, toast two slices of ______ . 먼저, 식빵 두 조각을 구워.

3. Spread ______ on them. 그것들에 버터를 발라.

4. Now, get a ______ of cheese. 이제, 치즈 한 장을 준비해.

5. This makes the sandwich ______ !
이것은 샌드위치를 신선하게 만들어!

6. Put it on the ______ . 그것을 상추 위에 얹어.

7. ______ it with a friend. 친구랑 그것을 나눠 먹어봐.

▸ 알맞은 단어에 동그라미 한 다음, 전체 문장을 따라 쓰세요.

1. This makes the sandwich (tasty / fresh). 이것은 샌드위치를 맛있게 만들어.

2. Add some (cheese / lettuce). 약간의 상추를 넣어.

3. Add some (potatoes / tomatoes). 약간의 토마토를 넣어.

4. This makes the sandwich (juicy / fresh)! 이것은 샌드위치를 과즙으로 촉촉하게 만들어!

5. Press gently and cut it in (whole / half). 그것을 부드럽게 눌러서 반으로 잘라.

6. Your (sandwich / toast) is ready! 너의 샌드위치가 다 됐어!

Sandwich ▸ 그림에 알맞은 단어에 동그라미 한 다음, 단어를 따라 쓰세요.

1

bread | ham

2

lettuce | tomato

3

cheese | lettuce

4

butter | bread

5

ham | tomato

6

butter | cheese

▸ 단어를 세 번씩 따라 쓰며 철자와 뜻을 익혀 보세요.

1

clean 닦다, 청소하다

2

factory 공장

3

meal 식사

4

order 주문, 주문하다

5

patient 환자

6

pick (과일 등을) 따다

▸ 문장을 잘 듣고 빈칸에 알맞은 단어를 써넣으세요.

work	water	clean	build
robot	order	patient	

P5.mp3

1. ______ s are everywhere today! 로봇들은 오늘날 어디에나 있어요!
2. Robots can ______ the house. 로봇들은 집을 청소할 수 있어요.
3. Can they help ______ s, too? 그들은 환자들도 도울 수 있나요?
4. Robots can ______ cars. 로봇들은 자동차를 만들 수 있어요.
5. Many robot arms ______ quickly. 로봇 팔들은 빠르게 일해요.
6. Robots can take ______ s. 로봇들은 주문을 받을 수 있어요.
7. They can also ______ plants. 그들은 식물에 물을 줄 수도 있어요.

▸ 알맞은 단어에 동그라미 한 다음, 전체 문장을 따라 쓰세요.

1 They do (many / much) things for us. 그들은 우리를 위해 많은 일을 해요.

2 Can they (play / clean) with kids? 그들은 아이와 놀아줄 수 있나요?

3 They can (work / help) doctors. 그들은 의사들을 도울 수 있어요.

4 They can (bring / carry) your food, too.
그들은 당신의 음식을 가져올 수도 있어요.

5 Enjoy your (time / meal)! 당신의 음식을 즐기세요!

6 Robots can (pick / bring) fruits. 로봇들은 과일을 딸 수도 있어요.

Places ▸ 사람들이 있는 장소에 동그라미 한 다음, 단어를 따라 쓰세요.

1

hospital house

2

restaurant bank

3

factory school

4

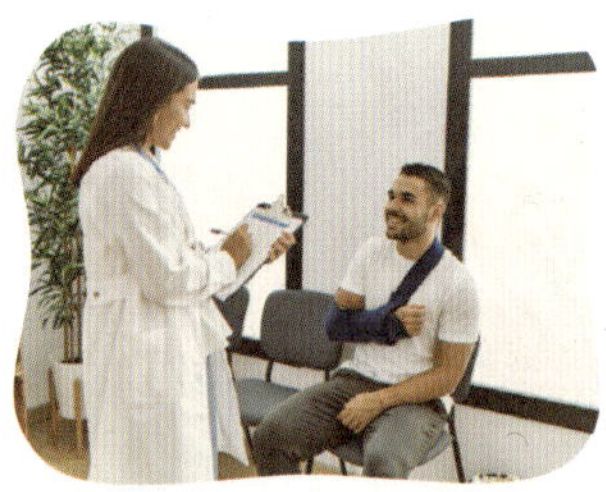

house hospital

5

restaurant school

6

house bank

▸ 단어를 세 번씩 따라 쓰며 철자와 뜻을 익혀 보세요.

1 

flour 밀가루

2 

grind (곡식 등을) 갈다, 빻다

3 

grow (식물이) 자라다

4 

hen 암탉

5 

plant (씨앗 등을) 심다

6 

wheat 밀

▸ 문장을 잘 듣고 빈칸에 알맞은 단어를 써넣으세요.

eat	wheat	enjoy	delicious
grind	herself	hen	

P6.mp3

1 Beaky, the little red ______, wants to plant seeds.

빨간 꼬마 암탉, 비키는 씨앗을 심고 싶어요.

2 The ______ grows tall. 밀이 키가 크게 자라요.

3 The wheat is ready to ______. 밀을 빻을 준비가 되었어요.

4 Who will help me ______ this bread?

내가 빵 먹는 것을 누가 도와줄래?

5 She works all by ______. 그녀는 모든 일을 혼자 해요.

6 It smells fresh and ______. 그것은 신선하고 맛있는 냄새가 나요.

7 She ______s the bread. 그녀는 그 빵을 즐겨요.

▸ 알맞은 단어에 동그라미 한 다음, 전체 문장을 따라 쓰세요.

1. I'm going to (plant / harvest) the wheat. 나는 밀을 수확할 거야.

2. (Nobody / Anybody) helps her. 아무도 그녀를 도와주지 않아요.

3. Who will help me (grow / grind) the wheat? 내가 밀을 빻는 걸 누가 도와줄래?

4. Who will help me (bake / take) the bread? 내가 빵 굽는 것을 누가 도와줄래?

5. Now Beaky has some (bread / flour). 이제 비키는 밀가루가 있어요.

6. I'm going to eat it all by (herself / myself)! 내가 혼자 그것을 다 먹을 거야!

Theme Words

From Seeds to Bread ▸ 그림에 알맞은 단어에 동그라미 한 다음, 단어를 따라 쓰세요.

1

flour / seeds

2

plant / harvest

3

wheat / flour

4

harvest / grind

5

bake / grind

6

seeds / flour

7

bake / harvest

8

bread / wheat

Practice Book 정답

Unit 1

p.3

Listening

▸ 문장을 잘 듣고 빈칸에 알맞은 단어를 써넣으세요.

town small bread check vet fire station library

1. Sam is going to **town** with his mom.
2. They go to the **fire station**.
3. A baker is baking **bread**.
4. They go to the **library**.
5. Have you seen a **small** dog?
6. They see a **vet** there.
7. The vet is **check**ing Max.

Unit 1 3

p.4

Looking for Max in Town — Sentence

▸ 알맞은 단어에 동그라미 한 다음, 전체 문장을 따라 쓰세요.

1. Oh no, Max is (coming / missing)! — **missing**
2. A (librarian / firefighter) is carrying a fire hose. — **firefighter**
3. They go to the (bakery / police station). — **bakery**
4. They go to the (police station / fire station). — **police station**
5. They go to the (cat / vet) clinic. — **vet**
6. "He is (healthy / sick)," says the vet. — **healthy**

4

p.5

Theme Words

Jobs ▸ 그림에 알맞은 단어에 동그라미 한 다음, 단어를 따라 쓰세요.

1. **teacher** / baker
2. vet / **nurse**
3. baker / **police officer**
4. **bus driver** / baker
5. teacher / **vet**
6. **baker** / nurse

Unit 1 5

Unit 2

p.7

Listening

▸ 문장을 잘 듣고 빈칸에 알맞은 단어를 써넣으세요.

living room special blanket bathtub bed kitchen bubble

1. We have a big **living room**.
2. My room has a cool **bed**.
3. We have a sunny **kitchen**.
4. There is a shower and a **bathtub**.
5. I like to make **bubble**.
6. We have a **special** room!
7. It's Joey's **blanket** fort.

Unit 2 7

p.8

Our Special House — Sentence

▸ 알맞은 단어에 동그라미 한 다음, 전체 문장을 따라 쓰세요.

1. We like to (watch / see) movies here. — **watch**
2. We have three (kitchens / bedrooms). — **bedrooms**
3. We (cook / sleep) and eat here. — **cook**
4. It always smells so (bad / delicious). — **delicious**
5. We have a small (bathroom / bedroom). — **bathroom**
6. He likes to (play / make) there all day. — **play**

8

p.9

Theme Words

Our House ▸ 사람들이 있는 공간에 동그라미 한 다음, 단어를 따라 쓰세요.

1. bathroom / **bedroom**
2. **laundry room** / stairs
3. kitchen / **bathroom**
4. bedroom / **living room**
5. **stairs** / laundry room
6. bathroom / **kitchen**

Unit 2 9

Unit 3

p.11

Listening

▸ 문장을 잘 듣고 빈칸에 알맞은 단어를 써넣으세요.

inside outside stormy snow rainy kite sunny

1. What do you do on a **sunny** day?
2. I go **outside** and ride my bike.
3. What do you do on a **rainy** day?
4. It's fun to play in the **snow**.
5. I fly my **kite** in the sky.
6. It's **stormy** today!
7. But I can still have fun **inside**.

Unit 3 11

p.12

Hello, Weather! — Sentence

▸ 알맞은 단어에 동그라미 한 다음, 전체 문장을 따라 쓰세요.

1. It's (sunny / stormy) today. — **sunny**
2. I go (inside / outside) and jump in puddles. — **outside**
3. What do you do on a (snowy / rainy) day? — **snowy**
4. What do you do on a (windy / sunny) day? — **windy**
5. I hear (storm / thunder). — **thunder**
6. Any (weather / place) is good for playing. — **weather**

12

p.13

Theme Words

Weather ▸ 그림에 알맞은 단어에 동그라미 한 다음, 단어를 따라 쓰세요.

1. cloudy / **sunny**
2. **rainy** / stormy
3. **snowy** / windy
4. **windy** / cloudy
5. sunny / **stormy**
6. snowy / **cloudy**

Unit 3 13

Unit 4

p.15 Listening

▸ 문장을 잘 듣고 빈칸에 알맞은 단어를 써넣으세요.

butter slice sandwich share bread lettuce fresh

1. Let's make a sandwich.
2. First, toast two slices of bread.
3. Spread butter on them.
4. Now, get a slice of cheese.
5. This makes the sandwich fresh!
6. Put it on the lettuce.
7. Share it with a friend.

Unit 4 15

p.16 The Yummy Sandwich Sentence

▸ 알맞은 단어에 동그라미 한 다음, 전체 문장을 따라 쓰세요.

1. This makes the sandwich (tasty / fresh). — tasty
2. Add some (cheese / lettuce). — lettuce
3. Add some (potatoes / tomatoes). — tomatoes
4. This makes the sandwich (juicy / fresh)! — juicy
5. Press gently and cut it in (whole / half). — half
6. Your (sandwich / toast) is ready! — sandwich

16

p.17 Theme Words

Sandwich ▸ 그림에 알맞은 단어에 동그라미 한 다음, 단어를 따라 쓰세요.

1. (bread) ham — bread
2. lettuce (tomato) — tomato
3. cheese (lettuce) — lettuce
4. (butter) bread — butter
5. (ham) tomato — ham
6. butter (cheese) — cheese

Unit 4 17

Unit 5

p.19 Listening

▸ 문장을 잘 듣고 빈칸에 알맞은 단어를 써넣으세요.

work water clean build robot order patient

1. Robots are everywhere today!
2. Robots can clean the house.
3. Can they help patients, too?
4. Robots can build cars.
5. Many robot arms work quickly.
6. Robots can take orders.
7. They can also water plants.

Unit 5 19

p.20 Robots Everywhere Sentence

▸ 알맞은 단어에 동그라미 한 다음, 전체 문장을 따라 쓰세요.

1. They do (many / much) things for us. — many
2. Can they (play / clean) with kids? — play
3. They can (work / help) doctors. — help
4. They can (bring / carry) your food, too. — bring
5. Enjoy your (time / meal)! — meal
6. Robots can (pick / bring) fruits. — pick

20

p.21 Theme Words

Places ▸ 사람들이 있는 장소에 동그라미 한 다음, 단어를 따라 쓰세요.

1. hospital (house) — house
2. (restaurant) bank — restaurant
3. (factory) school — factory
4. house (hospital) — hospital
5. restaurant (school) — school
6. house (bank) — bank

Unit 5 21

Unit 6

p.23 Listening

▸ 문장을 잘 듣고 빈칸에 알맞은 단어를 써넣으세요.

eat wheat enjoy delicious grind herself hen

1. Beaky, the little red hen, wants to plant seeds.
2. The wheat grows tall.
3. The wheat is ready to grind.
4. Who will help me eat this bread?
5. She works all by herself.
6. It smells fresh and delicious.
7. She enjoys the bread.

Unit 6 23

p.24 Beaky, the Little Red Hen Sentence

▸ 알맞은 단어에 동그라미 한 다음, 전체 문장을 따라 쓰세요.

1. I'm going to (plant / harvest) the wheat. — harvest
2. (Nobody / Anybody) helps her. — Nobody
3. Who will help me (grow / grind) the wheat? — grind
4. Who will help me (bake / take) the bread? — bake
5. Now Beaky has some (bread / flour). — flour
6. I'm going to eat it all by (herself / myself)! — myself

24

p.25 Theme Words

From Seeds to Bread ▸ 그림에 알맞은 단어에 동그라미 한 다음, 단어를 따라 쓰세요.

1. flour (seeds) — seeds
2. (plant) harvest — plant
3. (wheat) flour — wheat
4. (harvest) grind — harvest
5. bake (grind) — grind
6. seeds (flour) — flour
7. (bake) harvest — bake
8. (bread) wheat — bread

Unit 6 25

Story Reading

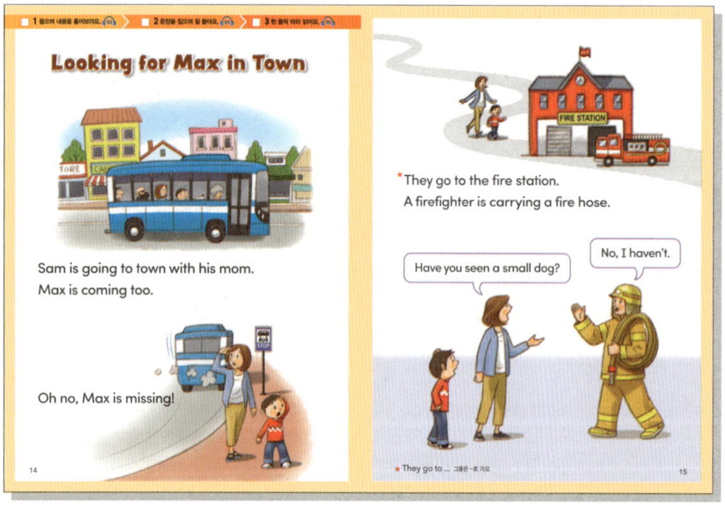

p.14

샘은 엄마와 함께 시내에 가고 있어요.
맥스도 함께 가요.
오 안돼, 맥스가 없어졌어요!

p.15

그들은 소방서로 가요.
소방관이 소방 호스를 들고 있어요.
엄마: 작은 강아지 보셨어요?
소방관: 아니요, 못 봤어요.

Tip Have you seen ~?은 '~을 본 적이 있나요?' 라고 경험을 묻는 표현이에요.

p.16

그들은 빵집으로 가요.
제빵사가 빵을 굽고 있어요.
엄마: 작은 강아지 보셨어요?
제빵사: 아니요, 못 봤어요.

p.17

그들은 도서관으로 가요.
그들은 거기에서 사서를 봐요.
엄마: 작은 강아지 보셨어요?
사서: 아니요, 못 봤어요.

p.18

그들은 경찰서로 가요.
그들은 거기에서 경찰관을 봐요.
엄마: 작은 강아지 보셨어요?
경찰관: 네, 저쪽에서 한 마리 봤어요.

p.19

그들은 동물병원에 가요.
그들은 거기에서 수의사를 봐요.
수의사가 맥스를 살피고 있어요.
"그는 건강해요." 수의사가 말해요.

Story Words

town 시내	missing 없어진, 실종된	firefighter 소방관	carry 들고 있다
hose 호스	bread 빵	library 도서관	police officer 경찰관
vet 수의사	clinic 병원, 병동	check 살피다, 점검하다	healthy 건강한

Theme Words Jobs (직업)

teacher 교사, 선생	nurse 간호사	police officer 경찰관
bus driver 버스 운전사	vet 수의사	baker 제빵사

Answers

p.13

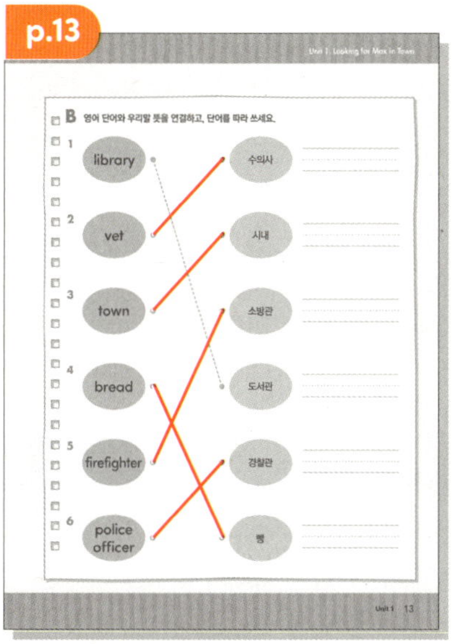

p.20

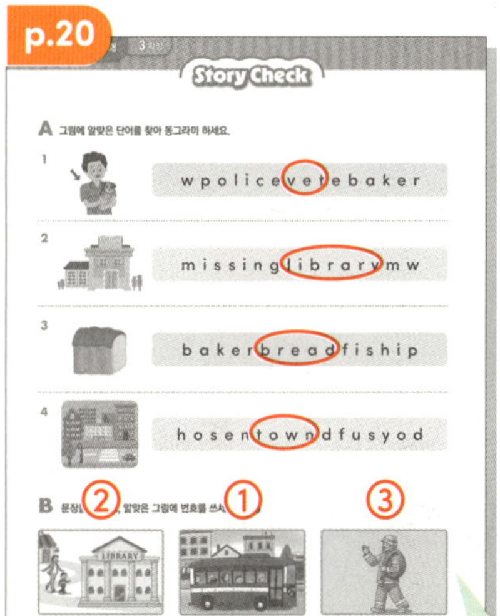

1. Sam is going to town with his mom.
2. They go to the library.
3. A firefighter is carrying a fire hose.

p.21

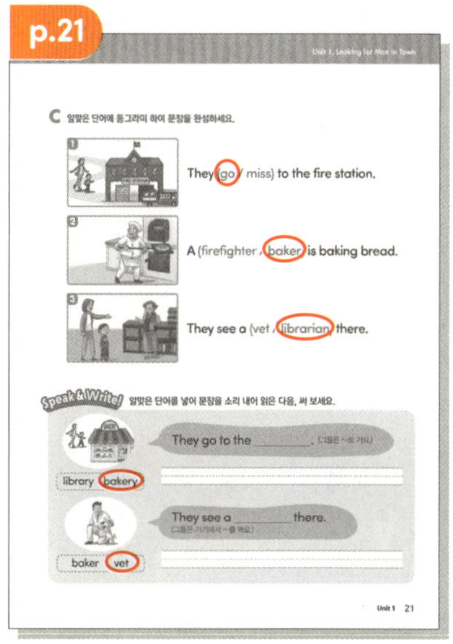

p.22

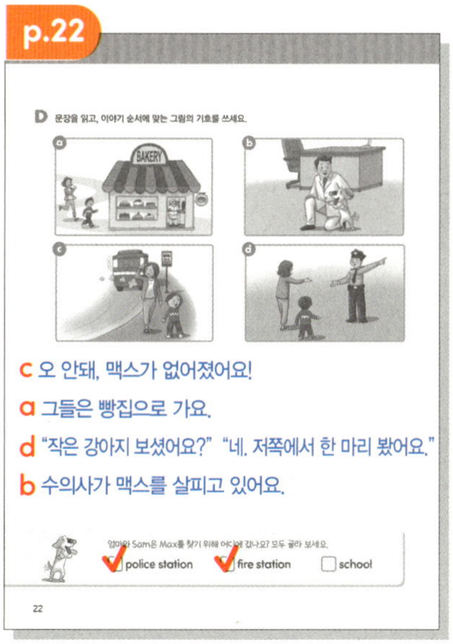

p.23

p.25

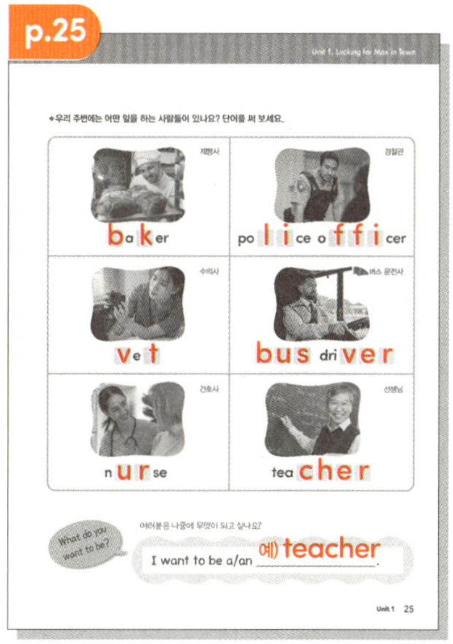

Unit 2 Our Special House 특별한 우리 집

Story Reading

p.30

우리 집에 온 걸 환영해요!
우리는 재미있는 방들을 가지고 있어요.
와서 보세요!

p.31

우리는 큰 거실을 가지고 있어요.
나의 가족은 여기서 이야기해요.
우리는 여기서 영화 보는 것을 좋아해요.

p.32

우리는 침실 세 개를 가지고 있어요.
내 방에는 멋진 침대가 있어요.
나는 여기서 우주를 꿈꾸는 게 좋아요.

p.33

우리는 햇빛이 환한 부엌을 가지고 있어요.
우리는 여기서 요리하고 식사해요.
그곳에선 항상 매우 맛있는 냄새가 나요.

p.34

우리는 작은 욕실을 가지고 있어요.
거기엔 샤워기와 욕조가 있어요.
나는 거품을 만드는 것을 좋아해요.

p.35

우리는 특별한 방을 가지고 있어요!
그건 조이의 담요 요새예요.
그는 종일 거기서 노는 것을 좋아해요.

Story Words

talk 말하다, 이야기하다	watch 보다	movie 영화	bed 침대
dream 꿈꾸다	sunny 화창한	delicious 맛있는	shower 샤워기
bathtub 욕조	bubble 거품	blanket 담요, 이불	fort 요새

Theme Words Our House (우리 집)

bedroom 침실	laundry room 세탁실	bathroom 욕실
living room 거실	stairs 계단	kitchen 부엌, 주방

Answers

p.29

p.36

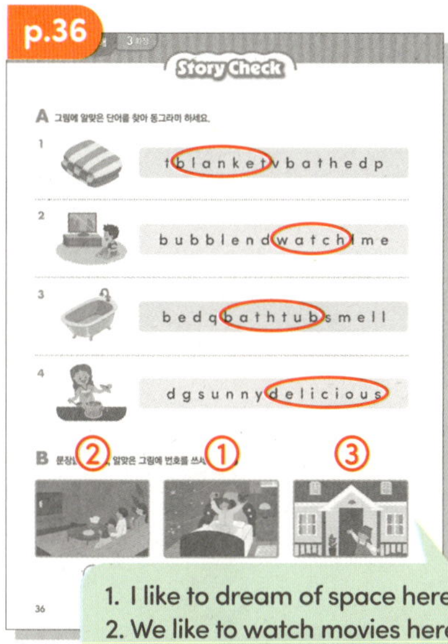

1. I like to dream of space here.
2. We like to watch movies here.
3. Welcome to our house!

p.37

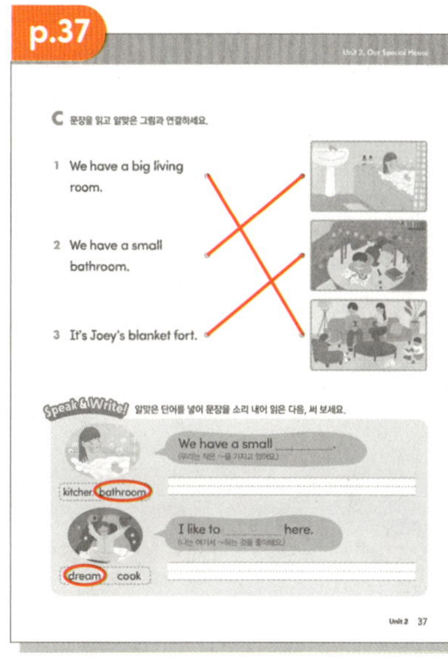

p.38

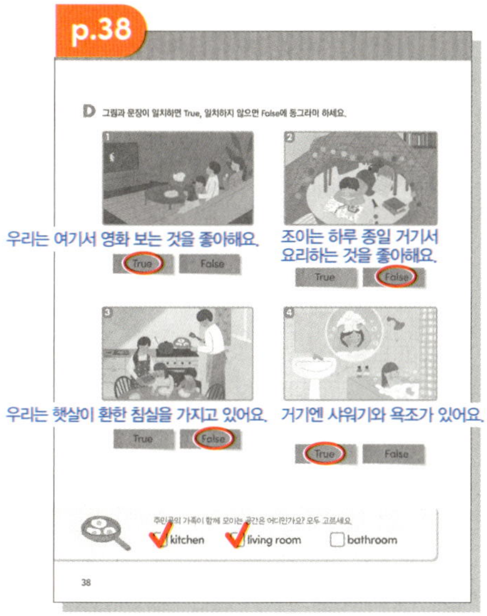

p.39

p.41

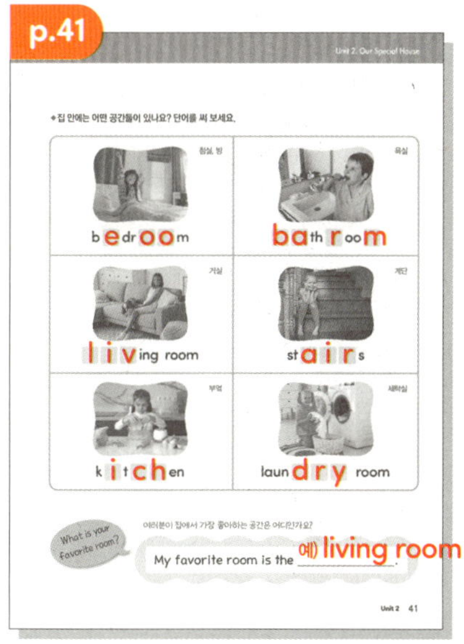

Story Reading

p.46

오늘은 화창한 날이에요.
화창한 날에는 무엇을 하나요?
나는 밖에 나가서 자전거를 타요.

p.47

비 오는 날에는 무엇을 하나요?
나는 밖에 나가서 물웅덩이에서 뛰어요.
빗속에서 노는 것은 재미있어요.

p.48

눈 오는 날에는 무엇을 하나요?
나는 밖에 나가서 눈 뭉치를 만들어요.
눈 속에서 노는 것은 재미있어요.

p.49

바람 부는 날에는 무엇을 하나요?
나는 하늘에 연을 날려요.
밖에서 노는 것은 재미있어요.

p.50

"쾅!" 천둥 소리가 들려요.
오늘은 폭풍우가 치는 날이에요!
폭풍우가 치는 날엔 밖에 나갈 수 없어요.

p.51

하지만 나는 안에서도 여전히 재밌게 지낼 수 있어요.
나는 읽고, 쌓고, 색칠할 수 있어요!
어떤 날씨든 놀기엔 좋아요.

Story Words

outside 밖에, 밖에서	ride (자전거 등을) 타다	fun 재미있는	jump 뛰다, 점프하다
puddle 물웅덩이	snow 눈	snowball 눈 뭉치	kite 연
thunder 천둥	build 쌓다	inside 안에, 안에서	weather 날씨

Theme Words Weather (날씨)

sunny 화창한	rainy 비가 내리는	snowy 눈이 내리는
windy 바람이 부는	stormy 폭풍우가 몰아치는	cloudy 구름이 잔뜩 낀

Answers

p.45

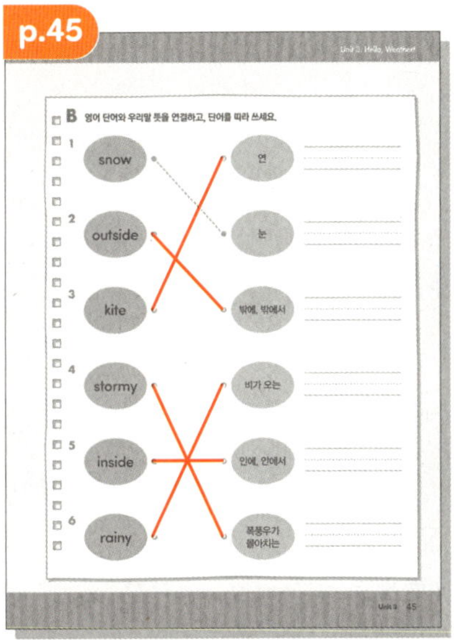

p.52

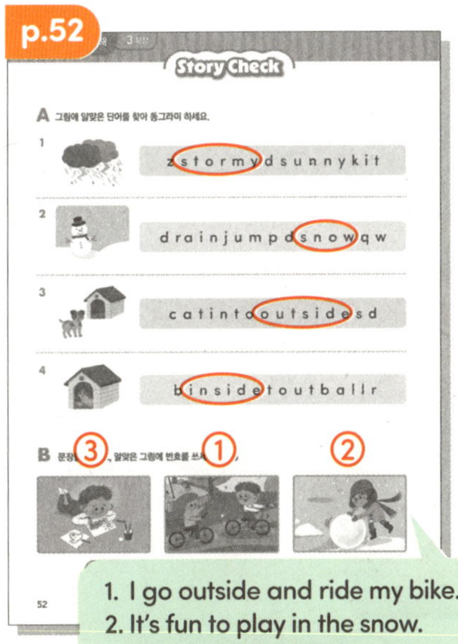

1. I go outside and ride my bike.
2. It's fun to play in the snow.
3. But I can still have fun inside.

p.53

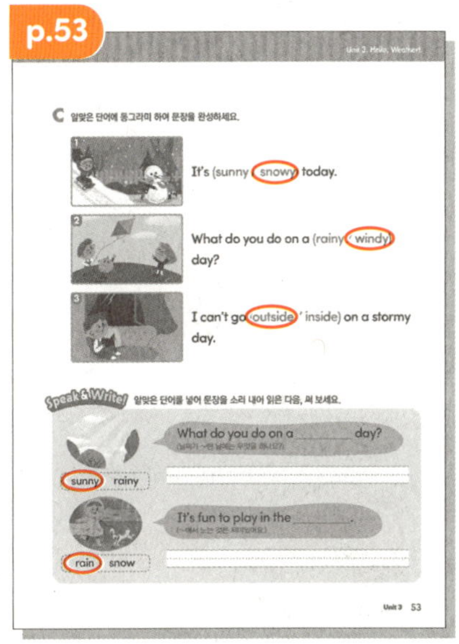

p.54

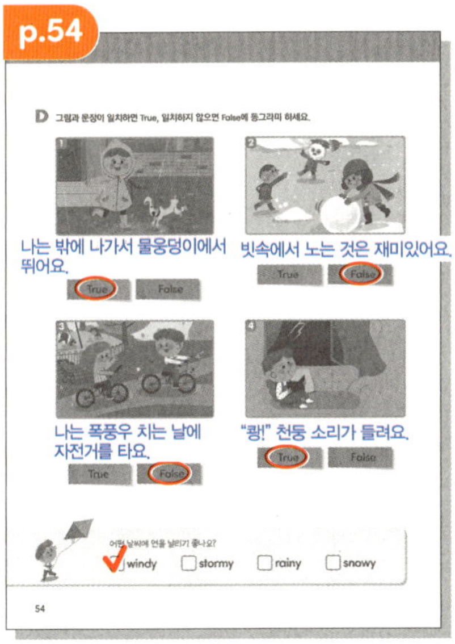

p.55

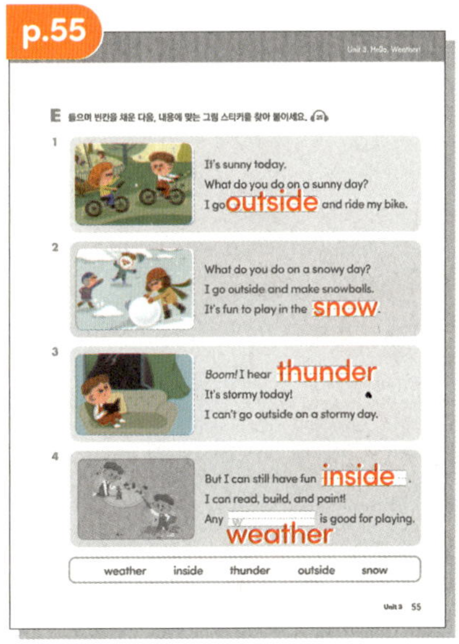

p.57

Story Reading

p.66

너 배고프니?
샌드위치를 만들어 보자!
그건 쉽고 재미있어.

p.67

먼저, 식빵 두 조각을 구워.
그것들에 버터를 발라.
이러면 샌드위치가 맛있어져.

p.68

이제, 치즈 한 장을 준비해.
그것을 빵 위에 올려.
약간의 상추를 넣어.
이러면 샌드위치가 신선해져!

p.69

그다음, 햄 한 장을 준비해.
그것을 상추 위에 얹어.
약간의 토마토를 넣어.
이러면 샌드위치가 과즙으로 촉촉해져!

p.70

다른 한 쪽의 빵을 갖고 와.
그것을 맨 위에 올려.
그것을 부드럽게 눌러서 반으로 잘라.

p.71

너의 샌드위치가 다 됐어!
친구랑 나눠 먹으렴.

Story Words

hungry 배고픈	sandwich 샌드위치	easy 쉬운	slice (음식을 얇게 썬) 조각
toast 노르스름하게 굽다	spread (버터 등을) 바르다	tasty 맛있는	add 더하다
fresh 신선한	juicy 즙(물기)이 많은	half 반, 절반	share 나누다, 나눠 먹다

Theme Words Sandwich (샌드위치)

bread 빵	tomato 토마토	lettuce 상추
butter 버터	ham 햄	cheese 치즈

Answers

p.65

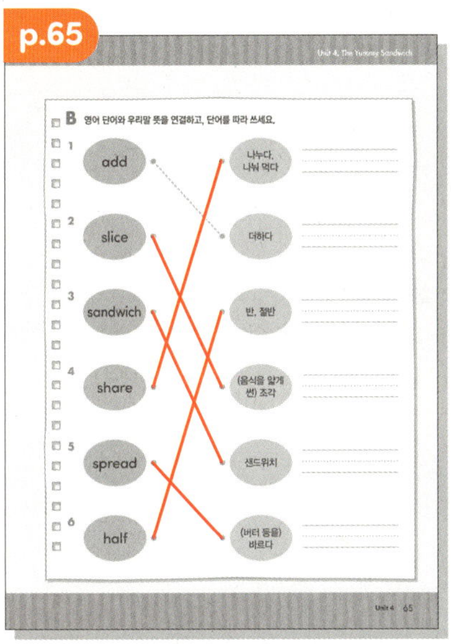

p.72

1. Let's make a sandwich!
2. Press gently and cut it in half.
3. Your sandwich is ready!

p.73

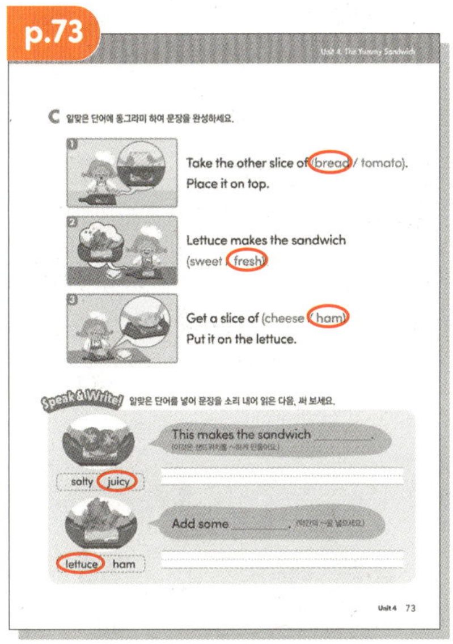

p.74

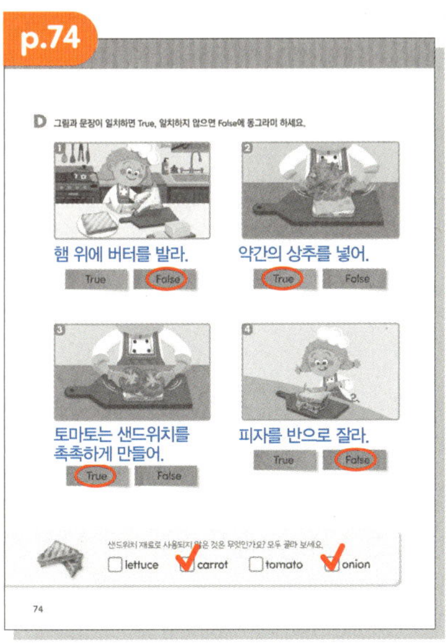

p.75

p.77

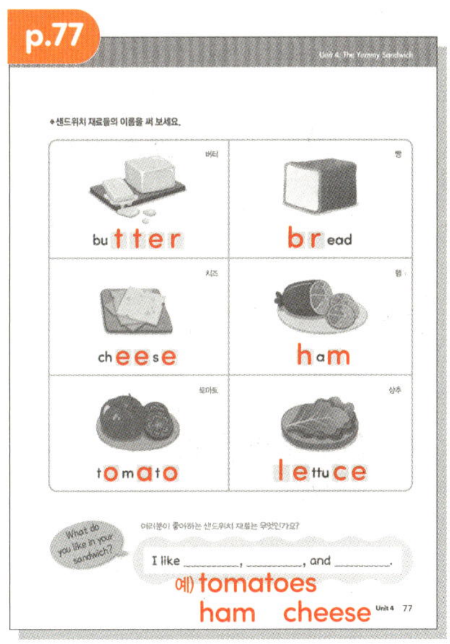

Story Reading

p.82

로봇들은 오늘날 어디에나 있어요!
그들은 우리를 위해 많은 일을 해요.

p.83

집에서

로봇들은 집을 청소할 수 있어요.
그들은 아이와 놀아줄 수 있나요?
네, 그들은 할 수 있어요!

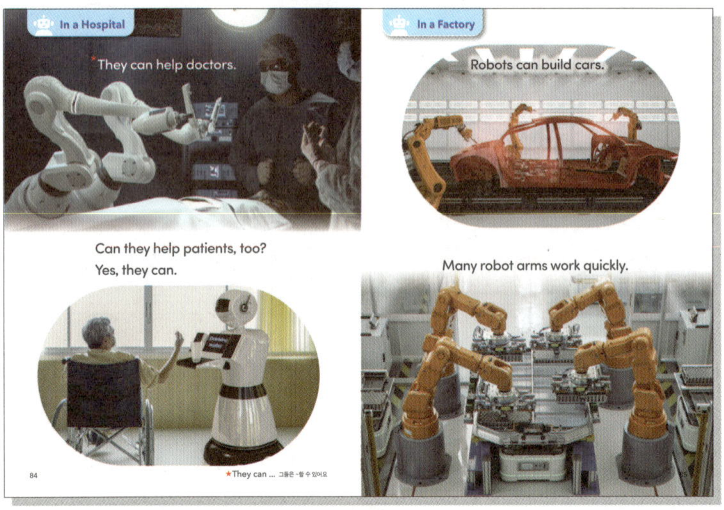

p.84

병원에서

그들은 의사들을 도울 수 있어요.
그들은 환자들도 도울 수 있나요?
네, 그들은 할 수 있어요.

p.85

공장에서

로봇들은 자동차를 만들 수 있어요.
여러 개의 로봇 팔들이 빠르게 일해요.

p.86

식당에서

로봇들은 주문을 받을 수 있어요.
그들은 음식을 가져다 줄 수도 있어요.
로봇: 맛있게 드세요!

p.87

농장에서

로봇들은 과일을 딸 수 있어요.
그들은 식물에 물도 줄 수 있어요.

Story Words

everywhere 모든 곳에	clean 닦다, 청소하다	kid 아이, 어린이	doctor 의사
patient 환자	arm 팔	build 만들어 내다	quickly 빠르게, 재빨리
order 주문하다	meal 식사	pick (과일 등을) 따다	water 물을 주다

Theme Words Places (장소)

restaurant 식당	house 집	factory 공장
hospital 병원	school 학교	bank 은행

Answers

p.81

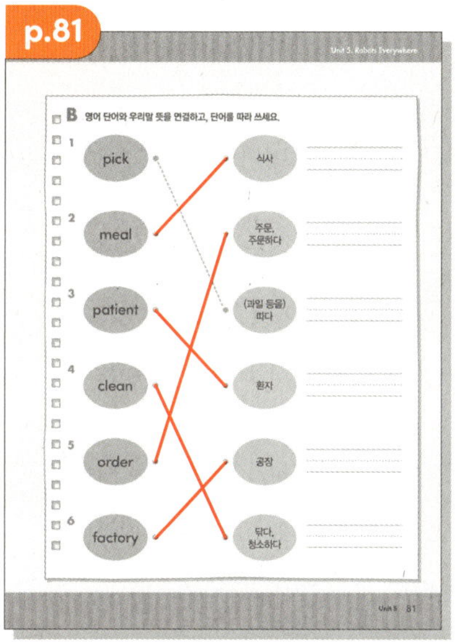

p.88

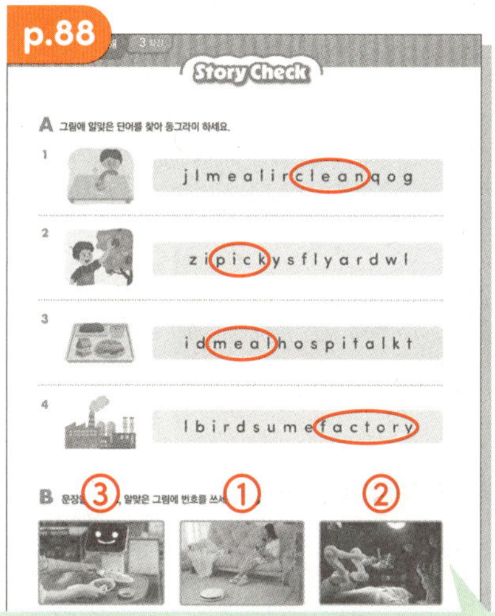

1. At home, robots can clean the house.
2. In a hospital, they can help doctors.
3. In a restaurant, they can bring your food.

p.89

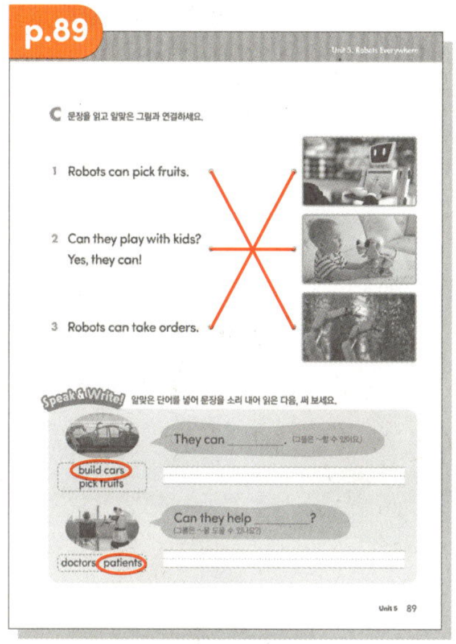

p.90

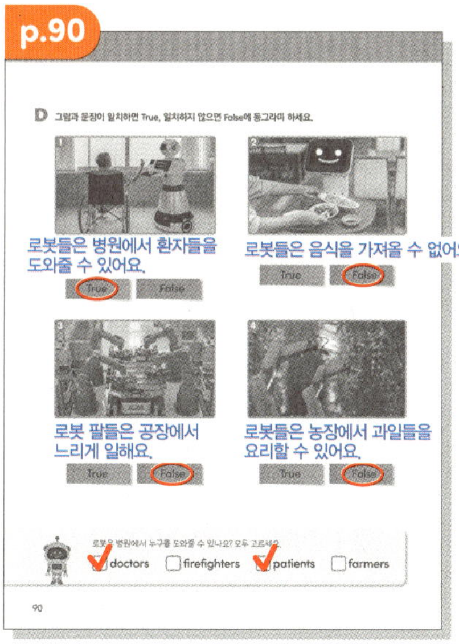

p.91

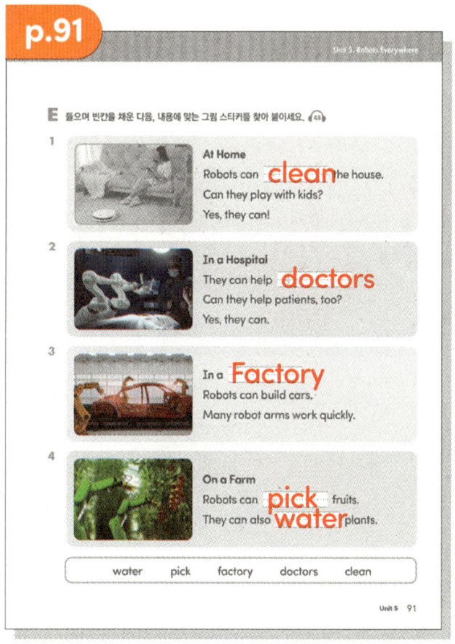

p.93

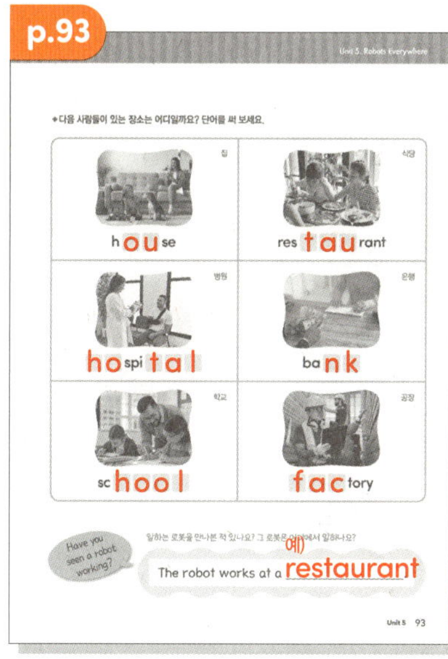

Story Reading

p.98

빨간 꼬마 암탉, 비키는 씨앗을 심고 싶어요.
비키: 누가 나를 도와줄래?
돼지: 난 아냐. 꿀, 꿀!
고양이: 난 아냐. 야옹, 야옹!

p.99

밀이 크게 자라요.
비키: 나는 밀을 수확할 거야.
누가 나를 도와줄래?
아무도 그녀를 도와주지 않아요.
그녀는 혼자 일해요.

p.100

밀을 빻을 준비가 돼요.
비키: 내가 밀을 빻는 걸 누가 도와줄래?
돼지: 난 아냐. 꿀, 꿀!
고양이: 난 아냐. 야옹, 야옹!

p.101

이제 비키는 밀가루가 있어요.
비키: 내가 빵 굽는 것을 누가 도와줄래?
다시, 아무도 그녀를 도와주지 않아요.
그녀는 혼자 일해요.

p.102

빵이 다 됐어요.
그것은 신선하고 맛있는 냄새가 나요.
비키: 내가 빵 먹는 것을 누가 도와줄래?
돼지: 내가 할게! 꿀, 꿀!
고양이: 내가 할게! 야옹, 야옹!

p.103

비키: 아니, 너희는 하지 마.
나 혼자 다 먹을 거야!
그녀는 그 빵을 즐겨요.

Story Words

hen 암탉	plant ~을 심다	wheat 밀	grow 자라다
nobody 아무도 ~ 않다	work 일하다	will ~할 것이다	by herself (그녀) 혼자 힘으로
flour 밀가루	again 한 번 더, 다시	who 누구, 누가	enjoy 즐기다

Theme Words From Seeds to Bread (씨앗에서 빵까지)

seeds 씨앗들	plant (씨앗 등을) 심다	wheat 밀	harvest 수확하다
grind (곡식 등을) 갈다, 빻다	flour 밀가루	bake (음식을) 굽다	bread 빵

Answers

p.97

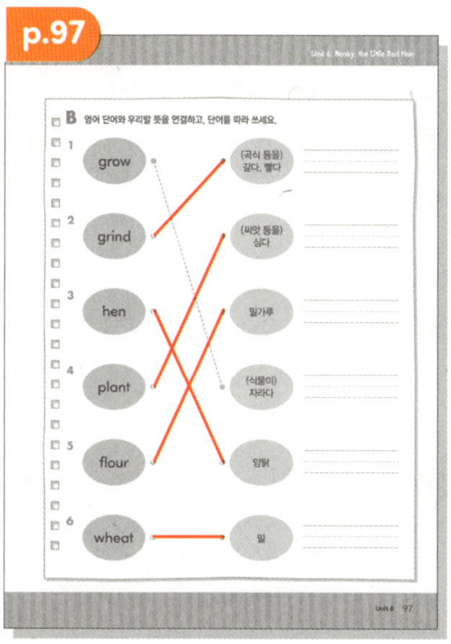

p.104

1. Who will help me grind the wheat?
2. Nobody helps her.
3. She enjoys the bread.

p.105

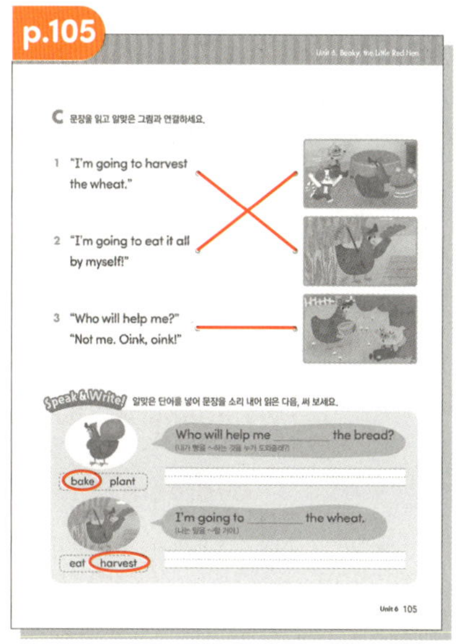

p.106

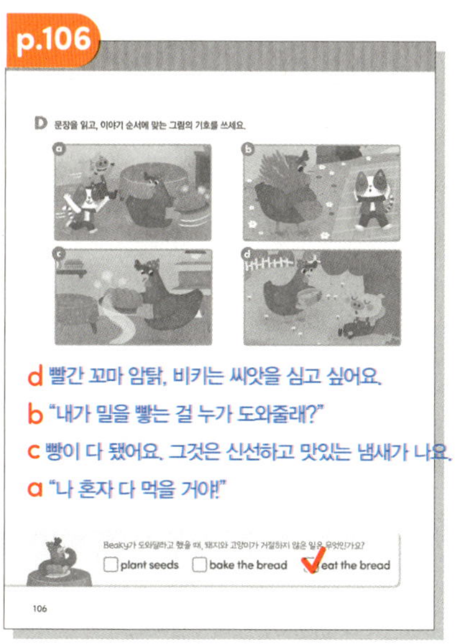

p.107

p.109

Review Test 정답

p.59

Review Test ❶ Unit 1~3

Words 그림에 맞는 단어를 찾아 쓰세요. (/ 10)

kitchen bread kite bathtub inside
vet outside blanket stormy library

1 bathtub
2 stormy
3 outside
4 bread
5 library
6 kitchen
7 kite
8 inside
9 blanket
10 vet

Review Test❶ 59

p.60

Comprehension A 문장을 읽고 알맞은 그림의 기호를 쓰세요. (/ 6)

1 It's fun to play in the rain. ⓑ
2 A baker is baking bread. ⓐ
3 There is a shower and a bathtub. ⓐ
4 We have a sunny kitchen. ⓒ
5 It's stormy today! ⓑ
6 A firefighter is carrying a fire hose. ⓐ

Boom!

60

p.61

Comprehension B 그림을 보고 알맞은 문장에 V 표시를 하세요. (/ 6)

1 ☑ It's Joey's blanket fort. / ☐ It's Joey's kitchen.
2 ☐ They go to the police station. / ☑ They go to the vet clinic.
3 ☑ I fly my kite in the sky. / ☐ I make snowballs.
4 ☑ I like to dream of space. / ☐ I like to dream of snow.
5 ☐ Do you see a small dog? / ☑ Have you seen a small dog?
6 ☑ I go outside and ride my bike. / ☐ I read, build, and paint.

VET CLINIC
No, I haven't.
What do you do on a sunny day?

Review Test❶ 61

p.62

Theme Words 그림을 보고 알맞은 단어를 빈칸에 쓰세요. (/ 9)

Jobs: ❶ nurse ❷ police officer ❸ teacher ❹ baker

Weather: ❺ stormy ❻ snowy ❼ sunny ❽ windy

Our house: ❾ kitchen ❿ stairs ⓫ bedroom ⓬ living room

62

p.111

Review Test ❷ Unit 4~6

Words 그림에 맞는 단어를 찾아 쓰세요. (/ 10)

add spread flour order half
factory wheat sandwich patient hen

1 patient
2 wheat
3 hen
4 add
5 order
6 sandwich
7 half
8 factory
9 flour
10 spread

Review Test❷ 111

p.112

Comprehension A 문장을 읽고 알맞은 그림의 기호를 쓰세요. (/ 6)

1 Robots can pick fruits. ⓑ
2 Beaky works all by herself. ⓐ
3 Spread butter on them. ⓑ
4 Press gently and cut it in half. ⓑ
5 Beaky wants to plant seeds. ⓒ
6 Robots can help patients. ⓐ

112

p.113

Comprehension B 그림을 보고 알맞은 문장에 V 표시를 하세요. (/ 6)

1 ☑ She enjoys the bread all by herself. / ☐ She shares the bread with friends.
2 ☐ In a hospital, robots can help doctors. / ☑ In a factory, robots can build cars.
3 ☑ Add some lettuce. / ☐ Add some tomatoes.
4 ☑ Place the other slice of bread on top. / ☐ Place a slice of cheese on top.
5 ☐ Who will help me eat this bread? / ☑ Who will help me harvest the wheat?
6 ☑ Robots can bring my food. / ☐ Robots can clean my house.

Not me.
Enjoy your meal.

Review Test❷ 113

p.114

Theme Words 그림을 보고 알맞은 단어를 빈칸에 쓰세요. (/ 9)

From Seeds to Bread: ❶ wheat ❷ seeds ❸ bread ❹ flour

Places: ❺ factory ❻ house ❼ hospital ❽ school

Sandwich: ❾ cheese ❿ ham ⓫ butter ⓬ tomato

114

"방법이 다르면 결과가 달라집니다"

리딩 실력을 껑충 키우는

기적만의 3-Step 완전학습

기적의 영어리딩

* 전문가가 설계한 6단계 리딩 프로그램으로 빈틈없는 영어 문해력 완성!